WHY CATS PAINT

A theory of feline aesthetics

HEATHER BUSCH

BURTON SILVER

Weidenfeld & Nicolson
LONDON

"In order for something to be so, we first have to think it."

Albert Einstein

First published in Great Britain in 1994 by
George Weidenfeld & Nicolson Ltd.
Orion House, 5 Upper St Martin's Lane,
London, WC2H 9EA.

British Library Cataloguing-in-Publication Data:
A catalogue record for this book is available from
the British Library.

ISBN 0–297–83351–0

Photographic assistance by Martin O'Connor and
Annelies Van Der Poel.
Technical assistance by Ian Biggs and Kriss Rose.

Typographical design: Trevor Plaisted.
Editorial direction: Melissa da Souza-Correa.

Originated, devised and designed
by Heather Busch and Burton Silver.

Compiled by Silverculture Press,
487 Karaka Bay Road, Wellington 3,
New Zealand.

Why Cats Paint is a registered international
experiment in inter-species morphic resonance
and is designed to test the hypothesis of formative
causation. I.E.# 644-38837-59.

Published with the assistance of The British
Council for the Promotion of Non-Primate Art.

Printed and bound in Hong Kong.

Frontispiece:
Orangello, *Beam Me Up,* 1982. Acrylic on
yellow card, 48 x 68cm. F. Norbert
Collection.

TABLE OF CONTENTS

FOREWORD

My late husband, Dr. Arthur Mann, has been credited with the discovery of representational marking by domestic cats but I don't think he'd mind me telling you that he was given crucial guidance by a couple of three year olds. One, a beautiful ginger tom called Orangello, the other, an equally beautiful little girl called Francesca.

In 1982, Arthur was staying with Orangello's owners, the Norberts, in order to study their cat's prolific marking behavior as part of his thesis on Feline Territorial Demarcation Activity. The walls of the big studio were festooned with Orangello's colorful works, each one carefully labelled as to where and when it was done, the medium used, the time taken, and the ratio of verticals to horizontals. But after five months, he was no closer to any coherent explanation.

It was the Norbert's three-year-old daughter who broke the code. Lying on the floor one afternoon, sucking her bottle and looking back over her head, she pointed at a painting and said, "Moo-cow!" And, "That moo too!" Later in the day, when she walked back in, Arthur playfully asked her to point out the moo-cows again. At first Francesca just stared blankly, but then, twisting her head round to look at the pictures upside-down, she quickly identified them both. Intrigued, Arthur tried doing the same and was amazed to find crude but recognizable images of familiar objects in the house, like the large wooden cow that was used as a door-stop. Orangello was painting real things upside-down!

At last, cat painting could cease to be dismissed as some kind of instinctive territorial marking behavior and begin to be seen as a pre-planned communication. Just what that communication is and what the motivation behind it might be, can still only be guessed at. Had someone taken over my husband's research when he died, I feel certain we would know a lot more than we do today. But perhaps Orangello provided us with a hint in his last major work, *Beam Me Up* (see frontispiece), which he painted the day after Francesca's little toy Scottie dog was irretrievably lost down an old well. To us, it is a lyrical and well-balanced work, suggestive perhaps of flowers on a spring day, or an after-banquet fluttering of peacock feathers, but to Francesca, who lost no time in looking at it upside down, it revealed the unmistakable pointy ears and snub nose of her beloved Scottie.

Nora Mann

Left:
Orangello pauses during an invertist painting of dahlias to observe a tame parrot, which has just landed. While Orangello did not chase the parrot, he was obviously put off by its presence and later destroyed the work with obliterative lines. This strongly suggests the painting was a mood piece rather than a representational work. Either way, it represents a great loss given that photographically verified cat paintings can fetch prices in excess of $15,000.

PREFACE

Can you see the cat's tail? We so seldom consider the feline origins of the question mark that this old written riddle still puzzles children and adults the world over. Cats use tail signals to indicate their changing moods and perceptions, and because ancient civilizations accepted that cats had special knowledge, these signals were considered important and incorporated into the earliest forms of calligraphy. Thus, the classical curled-over tail of the curious cat is still found in most of our written texts as the symbol used to denote a question. It is our hope that by exploring the signs a small number of domestic cats continue to make today, we may rekindle an interest in their unique way of perceiving the world and perhaps derive valuable insights from it.

We are well aware that we can never communicate with cats, or they with us, on anything like the level we can with members of our own species. While great strides are being made in teaching dolphins and chimpanzees to recognize and respond to our commands, there still remains an enormous gulf in understanding. This is not helped by the fact that almost all attempts to analyze the way in which animals perceive their environment have been undertaken within a strict scientific context.

While readily admitting to the value of such study, it is the contention of this book that we may discover more about the perceptions of the domestic cat by examining its marking behavior within an artistic rather than scientific framework. According to biologists for example, human art arose out of man's early need to mark his territory and possessions in order that his ownership could be asserted and recognized by others. In support of their case, they point out that art is almost never considered on its own merit without taking into account the name of the artist. So whether it be graffiti in a subway or a retrospective at MOMA, art is described by biologists as being simply the end product of man's strong individual desire for status and acceptance within the group.

When you consider how much more art is than that, and what it has done to benefit mankind and tell us about the world, you will understand why we do not wish to allow our perception of cat painting to continue to be limited by an exclusively scientific analysis.

While theories on the aesthetics of non-primate signing are hardly new, we are aware that the great popularity of the domestic cat as a pet means any attempt to describe their marks as art carries with it certain dangers. The growing commercial value of cat art for example, has led not only to some misguided breeding programs (notably with Persians in Australia),

Above:
The classical curled-over tail of the curious cat which gave rise to our question mark, right down to the dot at the bottom.

but also to a few, thankfully rare cases, where cats have been trained to 'paint' for reward. To the expert eye, the resulting works inevitably lack any integrity and are easily spotted, but, because they can be photographically verified, an increasing number are creeping onto world markets and being snapped up by gullible cat and art lovers alike. These sort of practices may promote tremendous public interest and debate but, in the end, they have a negative effect, and the potentially important messages inherent in each work are lost sight of amidst the clamor for commodification.

Because cat paintings can be so joyous and full of life, it is only natural that a great number of people will want to enjoy them. To this extent, commercialization of cat art is inevitable, and already motifs from cat paintings have appeared on fabrics, wallpapers, pottery and the like. It is now crucial we do not allow a wave of popularity to diminish the importance of cats' work and tempt us into removing it from the art context, where it can receive the serious study and protection it so richly deserves.

While we hope this book will inspire readers to carefully examine paw patterns in litter trays for examples of aesthetic intent, or leave a bowl of damp marking powder out by the refrigerator in case their cat may wish to express itself artistically, it is not our intention to give instruction on methods of encouraging cats to paint. This ethically difficult area is well covered by other texts listed in the bibliography. Nor is it our intention to provide detailed information on materials, techniques or compositional analysis. Evidence of one-point perspective in cat painting for example, is more appropriately the subject of articles in such journals as *Cat Art Today* or better dealt with in the excellent displays on feline perception at the Museum of Non-Primate Art in Tokyo.

Finally, we wish to acknowledge our debt to Specieism—that school which presumes aesthetic intent for the movements, marks or sounds of another species and then sets about interpreting them, without prejudice, in the hope of gaining new insights.

It is our belief that all species on this planet have an equal right to self-determination. As human beings, we must suppress our desire to see cats confirming our perceptions and values through their 'art', and, rather than attempting to determine the direction of their aesthetic development on our terms, we must allow those few cats who paint to develop their own special potential. Only in this way can we be certain they will be able to communicate their unique, undiluted view of the world and perhaps provide us with the clues we need to ensure the survival and future wellbeing of all species—provided of course we can trust them to tell us the truth.

Heather Busch and Burton Silver,
Wellington, 1994.

INTRODUCTION

One spring morning in 1978, two weeks after a discussion with a rather conservative colleague on what does and does not constitute a work of art, we received the snap shots you see printed below, of a cat 'painting' on a Russian television program. Accompanying them was a rather caustic little note saying, "I suppose this is art too, is it?" This was our introduction to the possibility that cats might actually be able to paint and we were all intrigued. Even for a trained cat, the designs showed a remarkable symmetry and certainly displayed that fundamental requirement of any art work—a potential for meaning.

On his return from Moscow we plied our colleague with questions about the cat, only to discover he could remember little of the program and, not being able to understand Russian, had no idea what it was about. He had simply taken the snaps in a fit of pique one night in his hotel room and didn't know whether the item was filmed in a laboratory, if a trainer was present, what night he'd seen it, or even the brand of vodka he'd been drinking. Our attempts to get information out of the Russian Broadcasting center at Ostakino met with a 'neyt' response and then, just when we were ready to give up, a friend remembered a letter to the *Folkestone Star* about a cat who did paintings on kitchen cupboard doors.

Thanks to the *Star's* excellent database facilities, we found the letter, written by a Mrs. M. Smith of Canterbury. Many phone calls later, we were actually speaking to her. Unfortunately, her Muffy had died three years ago, but some of his paintings were still on the wallpaper in the hall and her friend had a ginger tabby who did some very interesting designs on the refrigerator now and then. We would be welcome to come down and have a look. Seven of us crammed into Mrs. Day's kitchen the next weekend was far too much for Tigger. He wouldn't even come into the house,

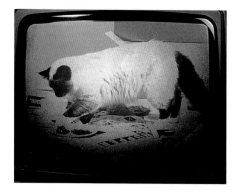 

let alone paint. But three weeks later, with just two of us present, we were rewarded with a brief yet spellbinding display of his artistry.

Tigger began by staring at the white door of the refrigerator for several minutes before stepping up to one of the saucers at its base and carefully brushing his paw pads lightly over the surface of the thick paint it contained. Then, perfectly balanced on his hind legs, he reached up and made the most delicate comma-like swirl of blue just below the handle. He repeated the motif three more times in different colors, one below the other, and then, with scarcely a glance at what he'd done, nonchalantly walked outside to wash his paws. The whole operation lasted only a few minutes but had been performed with such casual grace it appeared as if nothing unusual had occurred at all.

Many people have similar feelings the first time they see a cat painting. It seems such a perfectly natural thing for it to be doing that it is not until later they think to examine the cat's motivation—and when they do, the questions come tumbling in. Is it trying to represent something, an object maybe or perhaps an emotional state, and why? Could it be trying to communicate with us or another cat, or is painting a way of exploring its inner feelings? Do some cats actually have an aesthetic sense or is their 'art' simply a form of territorial marking behavior, as many biologists believe? We are much closer to finding the answers to these questions today than we were when we first saw those photographs fifteen years ago. A great deal has since been discovered about cat painting and we hope that sharing some of this knowledge with you now may give you insights that could help find solutions to the many mysteries which still remain—grinning down at us out of the branches above.

Below:
This cat (almost certainly a Birman), appeared on a Russian television program in 1978. Little is known about Russian cat painting generally and nothing is known about this cat in particular, except that the remarkable symmetry of its designs show it to be a highly advanced painter.

Chapter 1 | An Historical Perspective

In 1990 a dramatic discovery was made by an Australian archeological team working in the tomb of Vizir Aperia, just beyond the west bank of the Nile. Hidden for five thousand years in a previously unopened burial shaft, they found the embalmed and intertwined bodies of two female cats, Etak and Tikk. What was so exciting for Professor Peter Sivinty and his team was not the unusually ornate bronze and gold pendants that adorned their necks, nor the remarkable state of preservation of their non-mummified remains, but the fact that between the forelegs of each animal was a carefully rolled funerary papyrus containing the clearly visible marks of a cat's paw. These are the earliest known paintings by a domestic cat and the first conclusive evidence that cat-marking behavior was known to the ancient Egyptians and considered by them to be of spiritual and aesthetic significance.

The discovery of the Aperia Cats led to the immediate re-examination of other feline remains in museums round the world and resulted in a number of other funerary scrolls being found to contain barely discernible paw prints. Where these had previously been noticed they were usually dismissed as dirt or, in one descriptive paper, as "Single vertical smear (2.5 x 31.5cm) of excess embalming oil."[1]

But why were their paintings so simple? Why did they comprise of only one or two strokes compared to the far more complex paintings domestic cats are able to undertake today? The most likely explanation comes from Professor Sivinty himself. Writing in his book *An Epistemology of Cat-marking in Ancient Egypt,* he says, "...the cat of those times was probably just as capable of elaborate marking as our modern day cats, but as they were regarded as the medium through which the gods expressed themselves on Earth, it would have been seen as inappropriate for them to make a messy confusion of marks. What was required by the priesthood was a simple, unequivocal mark of authority. It seems most likely then, that once the cat had made its first one or two strokes, it would be considered to have finished and both the scroll and paint would have been removed." This view is supported by the Lapis Lazuli funerary scroll (right), where the cat is shown making a very bold paw stroke with great

[1]*Crighton, A.* Five Feline Funerary Figures. *Journal of Creative Egyptology, Vol. 44, 1951.*

Above:
Funerary Papyrus of *The Lapis Lazuli Cat,* Bodhead Library, Oxford.
Note the upright tail position of the painting cat, signifying its pleasure and therefore approval of the hieroglyphic text.

Left:
The Aperia Cats, c.3000 BC, holding scrolls, (Etak left), Phakat Museum, Cairo.

Above:
The Xois Cat. c.5000 BC.
George Young Museum, Berkeley.
This young unnamed female discovered
in the tomb of Nestpeheran on the island
of Xois, is shown here as she was found,
clutching the Xois funerary scroll,
(page 15).
In keeping with the scroll's message, the
cat's tail itself has been arranged in the
questioning form, with the tip ending on
the eye which represents the usual dot or
paw print that completes this symbol.

Right:
The Xois Scroll. c.5000 BC.
George Young Museum, Berkeley.
Here the mark of the curious tail has been
painted and then negated by a diagonal; a
sign from the gods that could be interpreted
as an approval to curtail a certain line of
inquiry.

confidence from a position directly above the Udjat, symbol of the all see-ing eye. Cats with their paws raised were always thought to be making the sign of Ra, god of the sun, but it is now clear that they are painting and the image of a painting cat is generally recognized to be a sign of celestial approval for the inscriptions on the scroll.

Some studies have suggested that the hieroglyphics on feline funerary scrolls may have been an explanation of the cat's painting, but written at a later stage by the priests. In the Xois scroll for example (page 15), we read, "...free us from the burden of questions, our trust goes forth without questions." Given that the curious form of the tail is so clearly represented in the cat's painting and then negated by a diagonal, it is argued that these words are too appropriate not to have been added later.

However, tempting as it may be to interpret them as one of the earliest known pieces of art criticism, there are several places where the cat's painting medium has clearly overlaid the human inscriptions, thus proving that it post-dated them. Indeed, if further evidence is needed that cat's marks were applied as a seal of approval, it can be found in the famous wall painting at Deir el Medina (page 16), where the cat's mark is clearly affirming of the propositions outlined in the hieroglyphic text.

15

a.

b.

c.

d.

Left: (a). The Udjat represents the all-seeing eye which can penetrate the higher spiritual realms that are unavailable to human beings. This symbol is often connected with the cat and can be seen in various forms on the scrolls and pendants shown in previous pages. Note that the eye of the painting cat is in the form of the Udjat.

(b). This grouping of symbols represents the Ebut or painting apparatus used by the cat. The two rounded shapes stand for two different colors of paint. To the left of them, the L-shaped symbol represents the combined easel and paint tray or Lex. Underneath is the stool or Poot on which the cat sits while painting. The Ebut signifies the means of affirmation.

(c). This is the Punkut which incorporates the dual sign of the curled-over tail above the oval symbol of Ru. Ru represents the cat's eye, doorway to the spiritual realms. The Punkut stands for the counterbalanced psychic perceptions of two cats, a kind of Yin Yang of spiritual inquiry.

(d). This almost totally obscured symbol is the Nildjat or "the contemplative cat who sits peering into the hidden realms of the spirit world." The Nildjat represents the triangular form of the cat when seated in the contemplative position with the tail held in the inquiring mode.

Far left:
A reproduction of the tomb wall painting at Deir el Medina, c.1250BC. Here the sun god Ra in the form of a cat completes what is almost certainly the sign of the curled-over tail and paw dot. This signifies spiritual inquiry and perception of the inner world. The cat's painting affirms the hieroglyphics below which propose that inner perceptions are better confirmed by two cats rather than one.

Right:
German story card depicting the White Queen and the wicked cat, Betrug, c.1430 AD. Katzen-Kunst-Museum, Stuttgart, (Room 17, third floor, case 5, exhibit 8.3). The cat seen here making marks on the Queen's robe with her rouge, is the only animal in German folklore able to make meaningful marks. Even animals imbued with magic powers always change themselves into a cat before marking. Betrug is really a bear (see text).

There is little recorded evidence of cats marking between 1000 BC and the Victorian era, other than a few examples during the Middle Ages when cats became associated with witchcraft and were killed in their thousands. Throughout history, cat behavior has been interpreted according to the beliefs current at the time, so once cats fell from favor their scratch marks and paintings, instead of being seen as messages from the gods, were taken as signs of the devil.

We find a graphic example of this in an illustration on an early German story card (page 18). Here we see the White Queen with her arm draped lovingly round the cat, Betrug, who is making marks on her robe with his paws. The mediaeval artist has left us in no doubt as to Betrug's character. His piercing eyes and pig-like nose give him a grotesquely evil demeanor, in stark contrast with the smiling and trusting expression of the Queen. In this old folktale (recently made into an opera by Kurt Pries), the Queen sends her cat out in pursuit of a wicked bear who has captured her daughter. The unfortunate cat is crushed to death by the bear, who then cleverly returns in the guise of the cat and tells the Queen her daughter has been imprisoned in a vast stone labyrinth. By wiping his paws in her rouge he is able to mark out a false plan of the labyrinth on her robe so that she will attempt to find her way through the complex of corridors and fall into a trap as she searches for her daughter.

Regardless of this being a folktale, there is a strong suggestion here that cats were known to be able to make meaningful marks with their paws. It is significant that no other animals in German folklore were able to do this and even animals with magic powers had to become cats before they could mark. There is an example of this later in the story when the Queen, who has of course become lost in the labyrinth and had both arms bitten off in a struggle with the bear (who has changed himself into a lion), finds her daughter in bed with a dog. Before she can do anything, however, the bear once more assumes the guise of the cat and quickly writes a word on the wall that so infuriates the dog he decapitates both mother and daughter before being finally killed by the bear who in reality turns out to be the cuckolded King. (In the end, justice is done as the dog was the queen's ex-lover and the King's son by a previous marriage).

A rare case of cat painting being seen in a positive light during the Middle Ages occurs in the Book of Kells where we find an illustration of a saint with the head and paws of a cat. It seems likely that this is Santo Gato (Saint Cat), referred to by Giraldus Cambrensis in his *Topographia Hiberniae* where he records the legend of a cat who, "...had many toes and did ably assist with the work of illumination." The cat in the Book of Kells does have extra toes (polydactylism), and it is probable that this oddity in one of the monastery cats, coupled with an ability to mark, would have led to its being venerated as a messenger of God.

Below:
Santo Gato or Didymus. Detail of original, 33 x 24cm, from Book of Kells, c. 900 AD. P. 48, chapter 17, St John's Gospel (St Columkille's MS). University of Belfast. A legend recorded by Geraldus Cambrensis in 1185 tells of a many-toed cat who assisted the monks at the monastery church of Columkille in Ireland with their work in illuminating the Book of Kells. It seems natural that monks who were cloistered away illuminating manuscripts would have enjoyed the company of cats, and as artists themselves, would have been interested in a cat's ability to make marks with the paints that were available. Given the monastic setting, it would also have been natural for the monks to give these marks a religious interpretation. Another suggestion is that the monks may have thought the cat was moved to paint by the intense nature of the holy influences surrounding it, thus confirming their own purity of spirit.

Right:
Mediaeval bestiary illustration, c.950 AD. 41 x 27cm. From a manuscript in the Bodhead Library, Oxford.

In this illustration, two cats appear like humans in an alchemist's laboratory. The caged bird and the sleeping dog, prey and enemy of the cat, are about to be transmuted into gold, represented by the rectangle in the background. Later they will be made into more moons, symbols of the cat's spiritual power. The cat standing at the easel has taken paint from the conical containers below and is probably drawing a plan of the method to be used. Such depictions of the cat involved in dangerous pastimes doubtlessly led to the expression, "curiosity killed the cat." A later illustration in the same manuscript depicts a cat holding a rat out in front of it and squeezing its back legs together in order to force blood from its mouth so it can use it as a paint brush.

The cat ceased to be persecuted as a witch's familiar in Europe during the mid eighteenth century and while it was safe from slaughter, its marking behavior now became trivialized in accordance with its new status as a domestic pet. Dr. Johnson, a cat owner himself, is reported by Boswell as making the following scathing remark to Hester Thrale, who was bold enough to suggest some form of communication in a cat's scratch marks on a wooden door. "Show me, Madame, one word of meaning in these scratchings and I shall find five and fifty volumes in the tangled mess atop your pointy head!" A clever put-down perhaps, with its oblique reference to witchcraft, it nevertheless shows that cat-marking was observed and thought by some to be a form of communication.

By the early nineteenth century, cats were popular in the lounges of well-to-do ladies and their marking behavior was encouraged as a source of idle amusement. Bowls of flour were provided for cats to dip their paws into and "...they did then make prints upon a black velvet cushion which were read with great cleverness by Madame Sloan as to our fortunes and to the accompaniment of much mirth."[1] This frivolous pastime inspired a number of purpose-made tapestry cushions with scenes of cats painting.

[1]*Mrs. Stantiloup in* Dr. Wortle's School, *a novel by Anthony Trollope. Blackwood's Magazine, July 1880.*

Below:
Tapestry Cushion, c.1856. 36 x 46cm.
Mary Morris Collection Ascot.
Amongst the well to do in the mid 19th century, cats were encouraged to make marks with flour on velvet cushions which were then read in much the same way as teacups are today. This practice led to the making of cushions specially for the task with appropriate tapestry designs of cats painting. The following well known children's rhyme also owes its genesis to this pastime.

Pussicat, Wussicat with a white foot,
On a black cushion your spotty mark put.
One dab is a "yes" and two is a "no",
Pussycat, pussycat, give us a show.

Above:
Bonnie, painting a wall. Boston, 1989.
Because of the abandoned manner in
which some cats paint, biologists have
branded their work as no more than an
"obsessive-compulsive play activity
which results in randomized marks of
no meaning whatever."

Chapter

2 | Theories of Feline Marking Behavior

Biologists have been reluctant in the past to concede that cat paint-ing could be aesthetically motivated, preferring instead to explain it either as a form of instinctive territorial marking behavior, or as the playful release of nervous energy. Those holding this latter view cite the "...abandoned manner in which some cats pounce at the canvas allow-ing paint to fly in all directions..." as evidence of what is, "...no more than obsessive-compulsive play activity resulting in randomized marks of no meaning whatever."[1] However, to be consistent in this line of reasoning would require us to reject a good deal of human Action Painting as well. The work of Jackson Pollock, Willem de Kooning and many other abstract expressionists, could be dismissed on similar grounds.

A more substantial case is made by those biologists who suggest that cat-marking behavior is territorially based. They point out that domestic cats rely not just on the scent of their feces to mark their territory but also physically mark its position with carefully 'drawn' lines radiating out from it. We've all seen how cats do this; carefully scraping long grooves in the

Above:
Cats not only rely on the scent of their feces to demarcate their territory but also physically mark its position by carefully 'drawing' lines that point towards it like a large arrowhead. These are clearly visible to other cats long after the scent has faded.

Above & right:
The cat uses the soil that remains on its paw to make even more visible territorial marks higher up on the tree trunk. This type of instinctive vertical marking behavior is thought to have laid the biological founda-tions for cat painting.

[1]*Gimlet, M. The Mentality of Cats. XVth International Congress of Art and Nature, Oslo. 1988.*

Above:
Pinkle, a female Rex, very methodically sorts all the magnetic letters on the refrigerator into color groups. Whether colors have specific meanings for cats is not known, but it is clear they can differentiate between the main color groups and that a few 'enjoy' manipulating them. Attempts to compare this manipulation of ready-made objects to the work of Marcel Duchamp do not stand serious examination.

Right:
Pinkle, *Red Letter Day*, 1992. Plastic letters on refrigerator, 52 x 78cm. Photographic collection, Museum of Non Primate Art, Tokyo. After 45 minutes of very slow and careful sorting, Pinkle completes her work by pulling all the red letters onto the top of the refrigerator. This seems to be an entirely self-rewarding activity, for despite encouragement from her owner she will only do it when *she* wants to and there appears to be no other reason for her to sort the letters into color groups other than the obvious aesthetic 'pleasure' she derives from it.

earth or litter that point directly to the feces like a broad arrowhead. This acts as a territorial marker which can be clearly seen by other cats long after the scent of the feces has faded. To further extend this demarcation some cats will use the earth that remains on their paws to make even more visible marks higher up on a nearby vertical surface such as a tree trunk or wall.

Biologists argue that cat painting is merely an extension of this instinctive vertical marking activity. Asked to explain the motivation behind it, they claim cats are stimulated to mark by the odor of ammonia salts used as a drying agent in acrylic paints (cats will not paint with oils) which smells remarkably similar to their urine. However while it is reasonable to assume that the cat's instinctive need to mark its territory may have laid the foundations for its painting behavior, the major reason cats paint today appears to be largely aesthetic.

We shall never know the origin of the primal feline aesthetic gesture but it seems that wherever domestic cats are well looked after and have little need to define their territories, their marking behavior tends, in some rare instances, to become what Desmond Morris (writing about chimpanzees), calls a Self-Rewarding Activity. These activities, "...unlike most patterns of animal behavior, are performed for their own sake rather than to attain some basic biological goal. They normally occur in animals which have their survival problems under control and have a surplus of nervous energy which seems to require an outlet."[1]

But cat painting appears to be motivated by more than the need to release energy, and, far from being the result of randomized pawings, is in fact the product of an ability to recognize and manipulate form and structure. For example, we now know that some domestic cats are able not only to distinguish between colors but seem to 'enjoy' making spatial adjustments to objects of different colors. In 1992, the *Guardian Weekly* ran a story on a ginger tom in Seattle able to sort jelly beans according to color,[2] and in San Francisco a female Rex will spend up to two hours carefully arranging magnetic letters on a refrigerator into groups of the same color. In both cases, the cats become totally absorbed in the task which seems to have no purpose other than the aesthetic pleasure of color grouping.

[1] *Morris, Desmond.* The Biology of Art. *London, Methuen, 1962.*
[2] *Whitlock, Ralph.* The Cat That Got The Beans. *Guardian Weekly, July 19, 1992.*

Above:
Studies show that cats spend about 3% of their play-hunting time lying on their backs looking at things upside down. A recent theory contends that this may be partly why cats invert objects when they represent them in their paintings - a practice known as "Invertism" which was not discovered until recently because cat representations are very basic and not as easy to recognize when inverted as more complex motifs are.

The fact that some cats are able to make representational marks was not discovered until quite recently, and then almost by chance. In 1982, Arthur C. Mann began an investigation into the prolific marking behavior of a ginger tom named Orangello who lived in Sussex (see foreword). Towards the end of his study, he happened to look at some of the paintings upside down and noticed that a few of the motifs bore a more than slight resemblance to objects in the house that Orangello saw every day. Further study in 1983 of a female tabby convinced him that some cats are able to make crude representations of objects but, for some inexplicable reason, always paint them upside down. Dr. Mann died before his research was complete and, even though he never came up with a satisfactory explanation for the phenomenon, he did coin the term "invertism" to describe it.

Later investigative studies by Dr. Peter Hansard working with Ching Ching in Cambridge (1987), and Dr. Delia Bird with Eliot in Oxford (1990), confirmed Mann's findings, though their explanatory material differs somewhat. Hansard favors a functional approach which takes account of the fact that cats spend about 3% of their play-hunting time lying on their backs looking at things upside down. By measuring their pupil dilation, he was able to show that cats experience a stronger state of emotional arousal at these times and suggests this occurs because "...the cat perceives the inverted object as something unfamiliar invading its territory and later paints and marks it in order to disarm it." The cat does this he says by "...first representing the object, or an aspect of it, in its unfamiliar inverted form and then marks it with the usual territorial arrowhead shape as it does when marking its own feces. By doing this, the cat claims the offending object as its own and thereby renders it safe by asserting its control over it."[1]

Bird, on the other hand, feels that invertism is aesthetically motivated. Her study found that objects which were subject to inverted observation by the cat were no more likely to appear inverted in its later paintings than other objects which it had observed the right way up. Furthermore, she noted that many of the marks Hansard would consider territorial, could just as easily be interpreted as a representational part of the painted object (see illustration, page 31). Bird concludes that cats may invert when making representational marks, "...in order to explore form and structure from a fresh perspective by emphasizing abstract qualities."[2]

Both points of view must remain open to conjecture, but it is interesting to note, in Bird's favor, that the well-known German neo-expressionist, Georg Baselitz (b.1938), also paints his motifs upside down in order to counteract conventional modes of observation.

While the establishment of a coherent theory of feline marking behavior is still some way off, it has been brought a good deal closer by the work of Dr. Peter Williams who heads the Department of Applied

[1]Hansard, P. Functional Invertism in Feline Territorial Demarcation Activity. *Jl. of Biometrics, Vol. 1, 1989.*
[2]Bird, D. Eliot and the Aesthetics of Feline Invertism. *Journal of Non Primate Art, Vol. IV, 1992.*

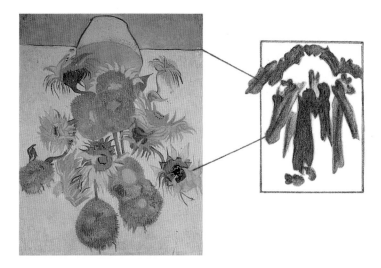

Above & left:
Buster's representation of Van Gogh's *Sunflowers* is a good example of invertism. From a purely visual perspective, the brown mark at the top of the work clearly represents the dark line which defines the edge of the table and the bottom of the vase, as shown in the photograph (left), while the blue marks represent the flowers.

However, biologists interpret these blue marks as territorial and similar in function to the arrowhead paw marks cats make to demarcate their feces. In the painting these marks signify ownership of the inverted object and are thought to have the function of rendering its unfamiliarity 'safe.'

31

Aesthetics at Rudkin College in Dallas, Texas. Evidence for an aesthetic motivation was predicated by a series of experiments he ran in 1987 to determine the degree to which domestic cats may display partiality for different works of human art. Because cats show a distinct preference for the works of Van Gogh, usually attributed to their being able to relate to the swirling fur-like nature of the brush strokes, Williams chose four posters of this artist's work and set them low on the wall in the cats' living space. By measuring the amount of time each cat spent looking at the different pictures over a six-week period, he hoped to be able to determine any preferences. The results were dramatic. All three cats, two female Siamese and a male Harlequin, spent 83.2% of their upright sitting time gazing at Van Gogh's *Sunflowers*. In order to check his results, Williams swapped the pictures around, only to discover that now the cats spent 81% of their time in front of *Café at Night!* A third swap six weeks later and *The Church at Auvers* became the favorite. What was going on?

"In experimental situations," Williams noted later, "you can become so obsessed with your hypothesis that the most obvious explanations completely escape you. I should have realized much earlier that neither the pictures nor their positions had anything to do with the cats' behavior. The fact was, that for some reason, they simply preferred to sit in a very specific area of the room which just happened to be right in front of one of our picture positions." It was also the way they appeared to be attending to a particular painting that made him think they were delighting in it. "They would sit there with their eyes half closed, purring and sometimes rocking slightly, though not asleep, as if the image before them was one of the most beautiful things in the whole world, as indeed Van Gogh's paintings are to us."[1]

A study by one of Williams' students who used tiny radio transmitters to track the daily movements of ten cats, found that four of them had

[1]*Private interview recorded by the author. Dallas, 1988.*

Above:
Maxwell, *Blossoms Blue,* 1991. Dye on
yellow card, 48 x 72cm. It has been suggested that this work may have been
inspired by Van Gogh's *Irises*, a print of
which the owner has hanging above her
bed, where the cat sleeps every night.

Above:
The typical pose of a cat when sitting at a
Point of Harmonic Resonance. The eyes
are slightly closed and the cat will generally purr and may rock gently back and
forth. Almost all cats that paint spend at
least ten minutes in resonance prior to
commencing a work, which suggests they
derive some inspirational power from
these invisible low frequency force fields.

preferred sitting areas that seemed to have little to do with warmth, scent or territorial observation. The cats would simply stop and sit in the middle of nowhere and begin purring as if they'd just been struck by the most delightful idea. The fascinating thing was, that at these times and only these times, small amounts of low frequency electrical interference were picked up by the transmitters the cats were fitted with.

It seems that some cats are able to experience a kind of localized force field or meridian in certain areas from which they derive a benefit. Peter Williams calls these areas Points of Harmonic Resonance and claims they may play an important part in motivating cat painting. It certainly appears that way with now four independent studies showing, that of the few cats who paint, almost all of them spend a large amount of time sitting in resonance immediately prior to painting.

Just why this should be so is still unknown, though it does appear that the cat derives some power from it. Certainly there are cats, often young and inexperienced ones, who will walk into one of these areas and become suddenly overloaded with a charge that's strong enough to make them dash madly all over the place. It may be that purring is a way of channeling the energy, or it could be a way for the cat to mimic the harmonic point's vibration and receive a kind of substitute benefit. At this stage it's all open to conjecture, but what is most exciting is that harmonic resonance could well be the vital clue in helping to explain what triggers the feline aesthetic response. Is it what inspires cats to paint, or do they paint its power? More importantly perhaps, could it be the influence of some intersection of lay lines, or something like this that causes us to see something in a certain way and make us want to paint it? It seems there may be much we can learn about the art of human beings by studying the art of the cat.

Right:
The fact that cats spend more time in our company than they do with their own species, suggests that there is something in their nature which echoes the higher levels of the human psyche.

Chapter

3 | Twelve Major Artists

Because this book is designed to function both as a work of reference and as an introduction to contemporary cat painting, it has been necessary to select only those artists who, in the author's opinion, best represent the major movements current at this time. Naturally this has necessitated some omissions and readers may be surprised to find that several cats whose work has risen to prominence of late are not included. This is usually because their notoriety is based on some particularly unusual technique or performance ability and is not representative of a movement or art-style as a whole. Also omitted is a quite recent 'trend' known variously as Fat Cat Chat, Claw Whore, or Neo-Felinistine. Time will tell if this peculiarly violent and destructive form of painting, popularized by the British and American Shorthairs, develops an integrity and viewpoint that would justify its inclusion in a future survey of this kind.

The actual number of known cat artists is still very small, with most being found in or near major cities where large populations can provide sufficient numbers to enable the formation of Cat Art Societies. It seems likely as interest in cat painting grows, especially in the newly 'awakened' areas of Eastern Europe, Russia and China, that many more feline artists will emerge with entirely new styles and messages. For this reason we cannot claim that the works included in this selection are representative of cat painting internationally. Rather, they show the important work of a small minority who are currently exhibiting and having their work sold in the West.

Almost all the works in this chapter have been given a title either by the cat's owner or its curator. The reason for this is straightforward. Just as surrounding a painting with an expensive frame and hanging it in a gallery places a value on it, so too, naming a work confirms artistic intent and allows it to be legitimated and taken seriously. Certainly, by titling a cat's painting, we provide a context within which judgements of aesthetic worth are made. A title such as *Fluff and Kittens* for example, is likely to suggest a different level of worth compared to *Maternal Arrangements* or *Coital Consequences # 4*. Be that as it may, titles nevertheless provide a clue, a starting point, no matter how arbitrary or contextually biased, from which to begin our journey of discovery. Without them, we run the risk of dismissing cat painting as being no more relevant than the mindless territorial daubing of the graffitist.

WONG WONG & LU LU

Duo Painters

Seeing Wong Wong and Lu Lu working together now, it is difficult to believe that their initial encounter was so filled with mutual hostility. Lu Lu (Luigi Vibratini Paletti), a Seal Lynx, had already established himself as a major Italian cat painter when Wong Wong, the lithe brown Havana eight years his junior, took up residence in an adjoining villa. Their first meeting on Lu Lu's Sansovino property near Bologna was witnessed by his owner, Sofia di Baci. Lu Lu was completely engrossed in painting the very large *Mural in White* (inspired by a distressing incident involving a row of milk bottles and the domino effect), when Wong Wong sauntered over from the shrubbery from where she'd been watching and calmly added a few graceful, paintless strokes of her own, just as if she'd been doing it all her life. The resulting confrontation left Wong Wong very much the loser (and very much the whiter). But as the weeks went by, her great interest, and persistent attempts to help, obviously impressed Lu Lu and led to her eventual acceptance as his painting partner.

Their initial collaborative works, *Breakfast for Dogs* and *Purr Balls,* 1990, lacked any clear direction. At over five meters long (down both sides of a Fiat Tempra station wagon), these murals were perhaps too ambitious. They lacked spontaneity, and Lu Lu's deft paw strokes were often confused by Wong Wong's exuberant introduction of irrelevant and poorly inverted material from unrelated experiences. While this added to the immediate lightness of the works, it tended to hinder their overall meaning. A far cry from their more recent work, *Wonglu,* 1992, the name signifying a deeper, more profound relationship and a unity of aesthetic purpose.

During the painting of this triptych, Wong Wong repeatedly stopped and rubbed up against Lu Lu, something her owner feels sure she did not only to gain guidance from the older painter, but also to share the works' progress with him on some kind of psychic level. This is borne out in her treatment of the large white form, which, according to critic Donna Malane, "… completely dominates the work and suggests a strong duality of positive emotion; 'giving,' shown at the lower open end of the white motif, coupled with a drawing towards 'accepting' in the upper moiety. The heavy, somewhat negative verticals in the left panel combine to echo this

Above:
Using his higher reach, Lu Lu completes the central motif of the *Wonglu* triptych by adding a few subtle 'off-canvas' smears. These action lines give the white form an immediate sense of movement which suggests a dynamic relationship.

Right:
Lu Lu signals his completion of the triptych by licking Wong Wong all round her face. Three days later, Wong Wong gave her final approval by making two black paw marks under the central motif, (page 39).

curl but the circle is tighter, less open and more selfish—the negative side of a working relationship?" Streaks of white were added to the uppermost tip of the dominant form by Lu Lu who has the higher reach. These "… action lines, give a definite sense of movement and imply an ongoing relationship." Lu Lu was content to sit back and wait for Wong Wong to complete two panels in her usual flamboyant manner before moving to add numerous bright little highly textured dabs of his own. These, according to Malane, "…have a diffusing effect, absorbing the dissonance set up by the conflicting messages of the first two panels."[1] An interpretation which helps to explain Wong Wong's need for a long comforting licking from Lu Lu on completion of the work.

[1]*Malane, D. Exhibition Catalog, New York. (While conceding that the central white motif does have strong emotive qualities, Ian Wordly, writing in the same publication, argues that it is more likely to be Tail Symbolist and therefore suggestive of the mercurial nature of their relationship).*

Below:
Wong Wong and Lu Lu pose in front of their parts of the *Wonglu* triptych. This work sold for $19,000 at auction in 1993, one the highest prices ever paid for a work of cat art. (Note Wong Wong's final two black paw marks in the lower left quadrant, acknowledging that the work is the result of collaborative effort).

In *Journey by See,* 1992, painted over five days on a brown fence, their two styles find a satisfying confluence. "The finely ridged, even grain of the painted wood reflects the light in web-thin strips that create a microcosm of silken threads, immediately recognizable as the sheen of Wong Wong's rich brown fur. The gaps (small), between the palings (broad), suggest both gaps in experience and collaboration. But these small voids are now triumphantly bridged by joyous shapes and colors that flow from board to board in a continuous reuniting dance of harmonic bliss. The once broken is made whole again."[1]

Much of their current work contains this simultaneity of romance and innovation. Here it awakens feelings and associations of renewal and completion with its free and open leaps of color across the fence. While in their latest work, *Galloping,* the same blend of energy and lyricism combines to create a work reminiscent of Kandinsky's *Romantic Landscape,* where cats ride horses in the snow.

Over the last few years, Wong Wong and Lu Lu have developed a close association with two horses. Alessandro, a twelve-year-old dark brown gelding, and Lolita, a four-year-old light grey mare. The association is at once symbiotic and aesthetic. On cold mornings, the cats will venture out across the fields and spring up onto the generous rumps of the quietly grazing horses. There they perch, receiving and imparting warmth. On balmy afternoons they may take long, slow meandering wanders over the rolling hills where, high above the ground, they can survey the land and discover new points of resonance. Each cat 'owns' a horse, and each is tonally attuned. Wong Wong to Alessandro, Lu Lu to Lolita, brown with brown, cream with cream, male with female, young with old.

But all is not harmonious. There is a subtle power play here. To ride the high horse, to maintain the equilibrium of feline dignity and independence, the cat must remain poised. The horse also has its pride to maintain. It chooses who will sit on its back and who will not. Both cat and horse have positions to defend. The horse can remove the cat from its rump (the most comfortable, least slippery spot for the cat) with one flick of its tail. But if the cat is not ready to leave, if taken by surprise and unable to remain poised, its claws will instinctively bite in. To avoid this discomfort, the horse must warn the cat, and that removes its power of surprise—its ultimate control. The interplay is delicate, the relationship both delightful and unsettling. The resulting painting is acute, and at times profound.

Galloping, 1993, painted on a green corrugated iron fence, is such a work. "The evenly rippled iron provides its own topography, imbuing the painting with an immediate sense of place. The undulating corrugations are at once suggestive of rolling hills—brightly lit tops and soft shallow valleys. The very evenness of the iron's form also provides a rhythm—the

[1]Hamilton, L. Italian Duo Painting 1990 -93. *Journal of Applied Aesthetics, Vol. IV, 1993.*

Following page:
In the summer Wong Wong and Lu Lu sometimes spend several hours a day on the back of their horses, Alessandro and Lolita. This is one of the few opportunities the cats have to move about several meters off the ground where resonances are more even and less prone to the harmonic surges encountered at ground level. For this reason, painting often follows these rides.

Left:
Wong Wong and Lu Lu working on *Journey by See,* 1992. Scented acrylic on stained wood. 974 x 87cm. Private collection, Bologna.

Below:
A preliminary sketch or dry-marking of *Galloping* made by Lu Lu three days before they commenced working on the mural. This alerted the cats' owners to the fact that they wanted to paint and allowed them to get the paints on site in time.

Left:

Galloping, detail, 1993. Scented acrylic on corrugated iron. 487 x 92cm.
Correa-Hunt Collection, Madrid.
White and black arched forms appear to gallop together over the regular green hill-like undulations of the corrugated iron. Lu Lu's delicate bursts of red and yellow overlay, complement (and correct?) Wong Wong's more gestural, less subtle treatment of the major forms, imbuing them with a sense of delight and movement. The crude starkness of the white figure has been given depth by overlays of gray which both soften and imply complexity.

Below left:

Interpretive Diagram, by Dr. L.P. Ashmead, for *Jl. of Applied Aesthetics,* Vol. IV, 1993.

1 & 4: Riding forms.
2: Bucking form.
3: Grazing form.
5: Butterfly (see detail, illus. opp).
6: Rearing form.
7, 8 & 10: Subsidiary shadow forms.
9: Leaping form.
11: Limb.
12: Signatory mark. (Wong Wong).

Ashmead's interpretation has been criticized by V. Hudson in the *Journal of Feline Art*, Vol. V, 1994, as being too contextually driven. She writes, "...while his interpretation of the work in the equine context is compelling, it suffers by being overly definitive. An equally convincing, though very different rationale, might also be found within a bovine context, for example, or perhaps vulpine, or cervine, or possibly porcupine, and even, might I suggest, Lichtenstein."

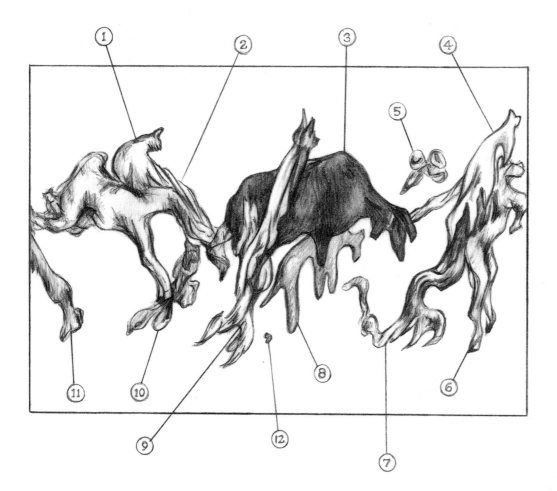

Left:
A touch of the old master. Lu Lu captures the essence of a butterfly in flight with just a few deft flicks of his paw. Later the butterfly is drawn to the likeness of itself and flutters around it for some time.

easy regular beat of horses galloping over the hills. Further, the deep shadows cast by each of the steel channels lend a definite sense of well-defined muscularity—powerful, boldly shaded legs that plunge directly into the ground—anchoring, stabilizing. It is on to this richly ambiguous surface that the paint is generously applied in long even strokes, at once reflecting and altering its inherent rhythms, capturing a sense of movement, a surging forward, cats and horses together in a joyously energized cavorting, that sweeps us up and takes us along for the ride."[1]

[2]*Downes, David.* Exhibition catalog, 1993. *The complete text of Downes' critique was first published in the catalog of La Expoizione dell'Arte Felino, Milan, 1993. It further explores the relevance of* Galloping *in establishing a feline-equine dynamic in the context of Trans-Expressionism.*

PEPPER

Portrait Painter

Pepper was born on a small farm near West Town, N.Y., in the fall of
1979. Being the only male in a litter of six undoubtedly precipitated a pre-
mature sense of his own uniqueness, and that, coupled with an umbilical
hernia at birth which required constant attention, set him apart from the
rest. As early as five weeks old he showed a tendency to be aloof, spending
long periods alone gazing at his reflection in the window and, more often
than not, content to sit back and observe rather than join in with his sisters'
play activities. It is not known who his father was but his mother, while displaying no artistic ability herself, was nevertheless a very conscientious
marker of the litter tray and it seems likely that Pepper's considered style was

Right:
Pepper will spend up to two hours carefully examining himself in a mirror before
commencing a self-portrait.

inherited from her. But it was the move to the Bacarella's spacious downtown Manhattan apartment with its large windows and broad sills that fostered a more profound fascination with his own reflected form.

His first work, with moisturizing cream on a dressing table mirror, was completed in 1981 and, while it lacked any clear form, this may have been because the smears were integral to the painter's own mirror image, without which they would make little sense. Later experimental work with facial powders and rouge, combined with some lotions, convinced his owner to supply him with the appropriate acrylics and during the next ten years, until his retirement in 1991, he painted over two hundred portraits.

Almost all his work involved self-portraiture and he would typically spend up to two hours carefully examining aspects of himself in a mirror before commencing. He then worked slowly, his painting seeming to inspire a considered awe as if he were overpowered by the enormity of each mark he made. Completion was inevitably prolonged, always requiring a final little dab here or there, several days after the main work was complete.

It was not until 1987 that Pepper showed any interest in painting Venus,

Below:
Pepper painting *Reflections # 54*, 1988. Acrylic on card, 72 x 48cm. Private collection.

"The relationship of self to a wider context is the antithesis of Pepper's works in self image which are iconographically firmly in the mould of egoistic self-portraiture. What is immediately engaging is the aspect of self image as represented by this detail of his tabby markings, not as they relate to the labyrinth of wider fur patterns but set apart, in clinical isolation where examination can be de-contextualized and deeply revealing."
Pott. T. Exhibition catalog, N.Y. 1990.

Pepper would often fight with his models during their painting sessions which his owner once explained as being because "...he just loses concentration and takes it out on them." A greater insight into this behavior is given by Dr. David Reynolds writing in the *Bloomsbury Book of Art* (1992). "The relationship between artist and model is complex. While Pepper uses his model's provocative pose to explore his own special reaction to it (and so gain a greater understanding of a special part of himself), he must also interact with her whilst painting in order to ensure she maintains the correct pose. This immediately exposes him to an external interaction which in turn compromises the purity of the internal dialogue he is attempting to comprehend. The resulting internalized polarity may explain the incidence of externalized physical conflict that often occurs during these painting sessions."

the Silver Tabby with whom he shared his apartment; and then it was with an impulsive enthusiasm as if he'd never seen her before. He would sit close to her for hours and purr loudly until she finally adopted the exposed supine positions he found so stimulating. Once she was suitably splayed, Pepper would immediately begin to paint. Now there was no pausing—his strokes were quick and vigorous as if speed were essential to capture the nuance of the moment (which in many cases it was, as Venus often tended to lose concentration and fall asleep in the more exacting positions). The

Venus adopts an advanced exposure position. On occasions she could maintain a pose like this for up to 15 minutes.

Right:
Exposure # 14, 1988, Acrylic on card. 72 x 48cm. Private collection.
Pepper perfectly captures the essence of Venus's exposed form. We immediately see the legs splaying out gaily from their central point of attachment, reaching up with an abandonment and optimism reminiscent of Susan Rothenberg's *Maggie's Cartwheel*, 1981.

resulting works are lyrical, every aspect of them exhibiting the undiluted essence of quadruped exposure. As Lesley Hertzog wrote on the occasion of Pepper's first one cat-show in New York in 1988, "...these works [the Venus Series] flicker between abstraction touched by the stability of the feline form and the feline form spiritualized by the undecidability of abstraction." He never reached these heights again. The onset of Venus's arthritis in the winter of 1991 distorted her lovely limbs and robbed his art of the stimulation it had come to rely on. After that, Pepper ceased painting altogether.

Left:
Tiger, (b. 1984), in his garden at
Königstein, near Frankfurt.

TIGER
Spontaneous Reductionist

The first thing one notices about Tiger's work is its unusual complexity. His multiplicity of colors, intricacy of line and constant variation of stroke angle to create texture result in paintings with a density of image unique among contemporary cat artists. Tiger's ability to manipulate colors was initially noticed by his owner, Elfie Henkel, in the garden of her Königstein property near Frankfurt in 1985. At first, the kitten's propensity to heap up fallen flowers or leaves into small piles seemed no more than a little unusual. Even the fact that he would sometimes carry a blossom in his

Eclectic Currents, 1992. Acrylic and paste on scratched satin, 64 x 47cm.
Dr. Philip Wood Collection, Berkeley. Because Tiger painted this on satin it would not yield to his reductionist intentions and, despite a good deal of clawing, maintained its basic form. This obviously annoyed Tiger, who, in the past, has been put off painting for months following misguided attempts to 'save' his work.

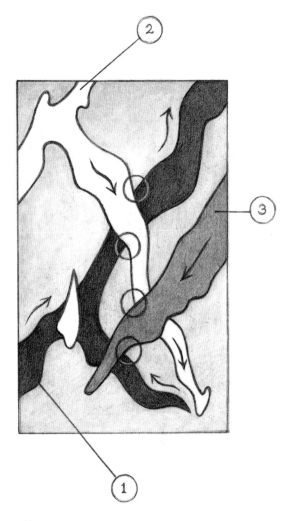

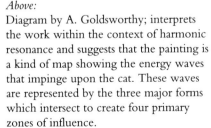

Above:
Diagram by A. Goldsworthy; interprets the work within the context of harmonic resonance and suggests that the painting is a kind of map showing the energy waves that impinge upon the cat. These waves are represented by the three major forms which intersect to create four primary zones of influence.

mouth from the other side of the garden to add to a pile when there were plenty of others closer, did not strike Frau Henkel as particularly strange. "It should have been obvious to me from the start," she said in a recent interview, "but because he loved to pounce on his little piles and destroy them the moment they were complete, it took a month before I realized that each pile was made up of flowers of just one color! One pile of five or

six camellias would be all red and another, all white."

What is so interesting about Tiger's recent work is that the same kitten-ish delight he took in destroying his flower piles, he now repeats with most of his completed paintings. But far from being simply a regression to an earlier juvenile play activity, it seems that his destruction, or rather 'reduction' has, and probably always had, a serious purpose. However, unlike other German Reductionists and Neo-Reductionists such as Puschelchen in Stuttgart and Miezekatze in Cologne, who express the

Above & below:
Tiger works vigorously, applying the medium across the three paper panels with quick rhythmical strokes that result in a pleasing textural complexity. He then removes the panels to reveal large areas of negative space onto which he paints his final motif.

reduced image directly onto the canvas, Tiger's method relies on the reduction of the completed work to the essence of its outer form. For him, art is not the reproduction of reality, but reality discovered through its reduction. It is this that makes his work more controversial than that of almost any other cat artist. As humans, we cannot fail to relate to its delightful complexity of shapes and colors, but equally we are puzzled, even appalled, at Tiger's sudden destruction of it. But rather than struggle to grasp its significance, Dr. David Hinds, author of *The Psychology of Feline Perception* (Berkeley, 1993) suggests an alternative approach. "Once we adopt the cat's mode of concentrated vision and stare directly into the void left by the removal of the painting's center, thus allowing the remaining form which surrounds it to enter our sight peripherally, we will perhaps begin to uncover the feline perception of reality."

Below:
The completed work, *Breakfast*, 1991. Acrylic and marking powder on card and wall, 184 x 86cm. Private collection.
In *Breakfast*, we immediately feel a strong sense of sadness—of something light and fluttering having suddenly disappeared—replaced by crude and indifferent smears that suggest greed and destruction.

MISTY

Formal Expansionist

Misty's popularity as a painter is due mainly to the figurative nature of her images. The elegant, bi-colored forms that sometimes extend up to ten meters in length, are immediately evocative and invite a wide range of projective interpretations. In a recent work, *A Little Lavish Leaping* (page 57), the surface is heavily built up with short black verticals to produce an elongated curvilinear mass that is at once dense yet strongly nuanced with

Above left:
Working with very quick strokes, Misty lays down the pink 'tension' areas first.

Above center:
The 'action structure' is composed of dense black verticals overlayed to suggest a series of interconnected curvilinear forms.

Above right:
Misty 'insisted' that the stool be placed in position so that she could complete the upper curved form to her satisfaction. Many of Misty's works go 'off canvas' and some, even go completely off the wall and onto the floor.

movement. Tension gathers at the base and builds upwards, flowing to a release (or is it a curtailment?) in the upper ovoidal form. What is so exciting about a work like this, apart from the obvious technical excellence, is its strength of imagery which, when combined with contextual uncertainty, encourages a high degree of varying interpretation.

For example, the cat's owner, Zenia Woolf, feels that the work concerns an incident in which her four-year-old son deliberately squirted Misty with the hose from the balcony. To her, each pink area describes the typical arched body of a cat as it leaps to avoid danger while the long black shape clearly represents the water snaking down from above and following the cat after its first strike, to hit it again—now more heavy and wet. Woolf feels sure the cat knew the work could not be understood if left within the confines of the canvas and when Misty was unable to mark higher than she could leap, meowed insistently for the stool to be moved so that she could complete the work. To her owner, the purpose of the cat's painting was to depict the distressing incident as clearly as she could in the hope that the owner would constrain the child from torturing her again in the future.

However, Michael Dover of the Orion Art Gallery in North York, who titled the work, has a different interpretation. He feels that it is too easy to find traumatic incidents in a cat's recent experience and use them as a context within which to interpret its art. For example, he correctly points out that Misty travelled in the Woolf's car to visit friends in Port Credit just a week before the painting was completed. On the return journey the son pulled her tail and was scratched on the wrist. Should we, he wonders, be interested in the fact that the form of the work almost perfectly describes that fifteen-mile stretch of coastline between Port Credit and Toronto, finishing with the shape of Center Island? Certainly, cats have a remarkable sense of direction but Misty wouldn't know that bird's-eye view unless she'd flown over it or had a long discussion with a local hawk!

Dover prefers to tackle the work from a more useful, functional standpoint and feels that it clearly describes some important aspects of feline leaping strategy. The curved black lines describe the path of the leap itself. It begins with the crouched form of the cat ready to spring in the upper right quadrant and follows it down to the pink impact-position below, from which it leaps again, to land with outstretched paws, in the next position.

Local art critic Emma Way agrees, but insists the cat is leaping in the other direction and that the pink areas describe the crucial spring-off points which dictate the success of the leap. Others have seen a dinosaur galloping to the right and there are those who favor a squirrel jumping down to the left. In the end we can never be sure just what Misty intended. The important thing is that we don't stop trying to understand.

Below:
A Little Lavish Leaping, 1993. Acrylic on card and wall, 120 x 170cm. Preserved *in situ* North York, Toronto. Misty's paintings are greatly valued for their strong yet ambiguous imagery which, combined with contextual uncertainty, allow for a great richness of interpretation. The power of this sort of cat art lies in its very incomprehensibility which enables it to provoke and intrigue.

Above:
Minnie, (Minnie Monet Manet),
(b. 1984), spends a good deal of time
contemplating amongst the vines before
beginning a painting. After a two-year
caesura following poor reviews in 1988,
she now paints as often as once a week.

MINNIE

Abstract Expressionist

As soon as Minnie left Lyon and went to live at the little vineyard in Aix-en-Provence, her paintings changed dramatically, and so did the reviews. In 1988, Paul Seuphor had this to say about one of her paintings, titled *Three Blind Mice,* exhibited at the Galerie Félin in Lyon. "Three dreary monochromatic daubs with single trickles of excess paint running from each of them are evidently meant to represent blind mice. Certainly, they have no eyes. Nor do they have ears, or legs, or whiskers or anything else at all except tails. Maybe one can forgive them their difference, but where is their life? Where is the action? Where is the farmer's wife with her big knife? We could definitely do with her to finish off these pathetically uninteresting little blobs of gray."[1]

Compare that to the review she received three years later for an exhibition of her paintings in Arles. "...her work emits a luminosity that cries out with exhilaration, mystery and revelation...her many colors and directions allow us to glimpse the inner feline reality."[2] There can be little doubt that the relaxed warmth and lush abundance of Provence worked its magic on Minnie, as did a certain British Silver Spotted Shorthair tom named Pierre (Pierre Miayler), who shares her new home. He doesn't paint, but with one of their kittens selling in Japan for $20,000 recently (twice what Minnie receives for a painting), he hardly needs to.

[1] Seuphor, P. Patte-pelue. *Exhibition catalog, Lyon, 1988.*
[2] Du Mombrison, Henri. La joie au cœur. *Exhibition catalog, Arles, 1991.*

Left:
Minnie paints with enormous speed and pixie-like vigor, scarcely pausing to consider the work until it is complete. Her paintings, which contain unusual horizontal marks, refuse to be contained by the need for conventional boundaries and overflow 'off-canvas' in a vital yet balanced manner.

Below:
Reindeer in Provence, 1992. Acrylic on gold card and black wall, 120 x 180cm. Collection of the artist.

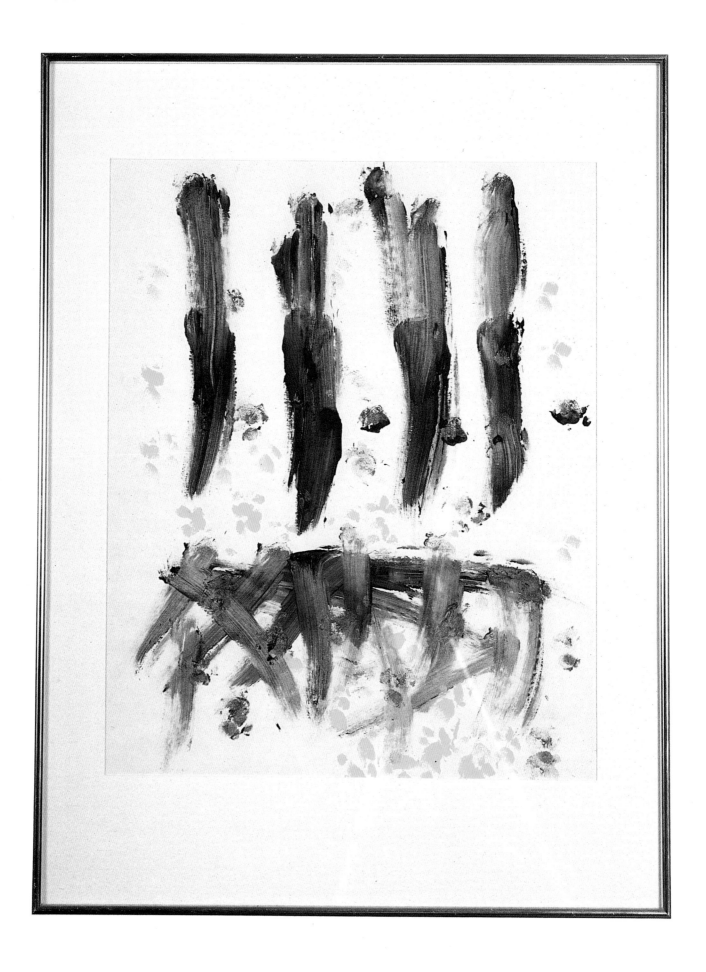

60

SMOKEY

Romantic Ruralist

Cats are the only animals other than human beings that regularly use drugs to heighten their aesthetic sensibilities. Smokey is no exception. His painting sessions are always conducted in a secluded part of the garden and inevitably preceded by at least an hour in the catnip patch. This explains not only the slow, almost ponderous way in which he paints, but also the remarkable depth of his pastoral vision. Of course, any artistically inclined cat living in the rural splendor of New Zealand's South Island, as Smokey does, could not fail to be profoundly affected by its clarity of light, its fecundity of image, its almost oppressive beauty.

Smokey has the ability not only to imbue his bucolic forms with elements of 'The Romantic' but also, more importantly, to maintain their dignity. We see this clearly in one of his best-known works, *Serious Ramifications* (left). "The first thing you notice about the work," writes critic Bevan Island, "is its bold regularity, its obvious symmetry. Not until

Left:
Serious Ramifications, 1992. Acrylic on board, 73 x 62cm. McGillicuddy Art Gallery, Christchurch. This study of a ram was originally titled *Ramshackle* by the cat's owner, but was later changed curatorially.

Below:
Despite the fact that Smokey (b. 1987) uses catnip or catmint (*Nepeta cataria*) before painting, her work does not reflect a psychedelic element. She seems to use it more as a way of intensifying the harmonic resonance experience which acts as such a strong stimulant to feline creativity.

Above:
Smokey, who can be seen in both pictures, studying and completing *Serious Ramifications* in the garden of his Nelson home in New Zealand's South Island. This study of Rodney, a fifteen-year-old ram, was the subject of a good deal of contention when it was purchased with public funds by the McGillicuddy Gallery in Christchurch for $6,000 in 1993.

later do we see the sheep walking. But once we do, the feeling of movement is powerful and immediate. We are able to peer through the confusion of moving limbs from a variety of revealing perspectives as it strides forward (right to left). Light flickers intriguingly as these oblique pediments divide and re-divide, impinging upon the dandelions beneath which appear to explode (implode?) under the impact. Now the four pre-eminent forms are at once the four hooves poised menacingly above; sharp, knife-like and ready to do battle with any insouciant tail or paw!"[1]

This picture has been the subject of much contention, with several reviewers taking exception to interpretations such as the one above which benefit from having seen the verifying photographs that accompanied it at exhibition. For example, as Dieter McLeavey correctly points out, "It is possible to claim almost anything for a work of art provided you can justify it contextually. If I say that the *Mona Lisa* is smiling at the ghost of her dead cat, you will very quickly find its spectral form just below her shoulder, even though you've never noticed it before. Could the fact that Van Gogh once shot a cat mean that the form in the bottom left-hand corner of *The Starry Night* is a cat sadly rubbing its eye? What is the significance of the slug-like cat in Matisse's *The Swimming Pool*? What if I told you he once drowned a sack of kittens?"[2] The point is well made. While the leap for a contextual answer, both as a means of understanding the work and relieving cognitive dissonance, is highly attractive, it cannot help but limit the scope of the painting and halt the essential process of exploration.

[1]Island, Bevan. Serious Ramifications at the McGillicuddy. *Christchurch Examiner, 1993.*
[2]McLeavey, Dieter. Strictly Ewephemistic. *Journal of Australasian Art, Vol. I, 1994.*

Above:
Smokey puts the finishing touches to
Manic Marigolds #17. He always chooses a
secluded part of the garden for his paintings and lets his owner know where to
leave his paints and easel by flamboyantly
marking the spot with urine.

Left:
Manic Marigolds # 17, 1991. Scented
acrylic paste on paper, 64 x 48cm.
David McGill Collection, Wellington.

GINGER

Neo-Synthesist

Above:
Ginger, (Ginger Katdinsky Kleeché Klipt), (b.1987), a sensuous cat who sometimes relates so strongly to her paintings that she rubs against them before they are dry, so inadvertently destroying them.

Despite showing early signs of an aesthetic marking ability, Ginger did not paint until she was four, and then only as a result of careful encouragement from her owners, Colin and Mary McCahon of Manchester. Her wallpaper scratchings had always exhibited a delicacy of line and a marked appreciation of surface texture, but she showed no inclination in those first years to explore the use of marking media. It was only after Colin McCahon had given her numerous demonstrations of how the damp sand in the litter tray could be used to mark the wall (thus proving to her that painting was simply a natural extension of her tray marking), that Ginger began to tentatively use the rich variety of scented acrylic pastes the

McCahons always left out for her. Now she is prolific, painting almost every day and often at night. Once a painting is complete, it is not removed, but left to act as a reference point for the next. In this way, her art becomes developmental, ranging widely over a variety of appropriate surfaces, including windows, curtains, tables, chairs and the occasional pot plant. The finished works are to be walked past, viewed sequentially like a story rather than experienced as a fixed single view in a fixed single moment—each painting existing as a memorable point on a continuum through which the identity of the feline self is slowly emergent.

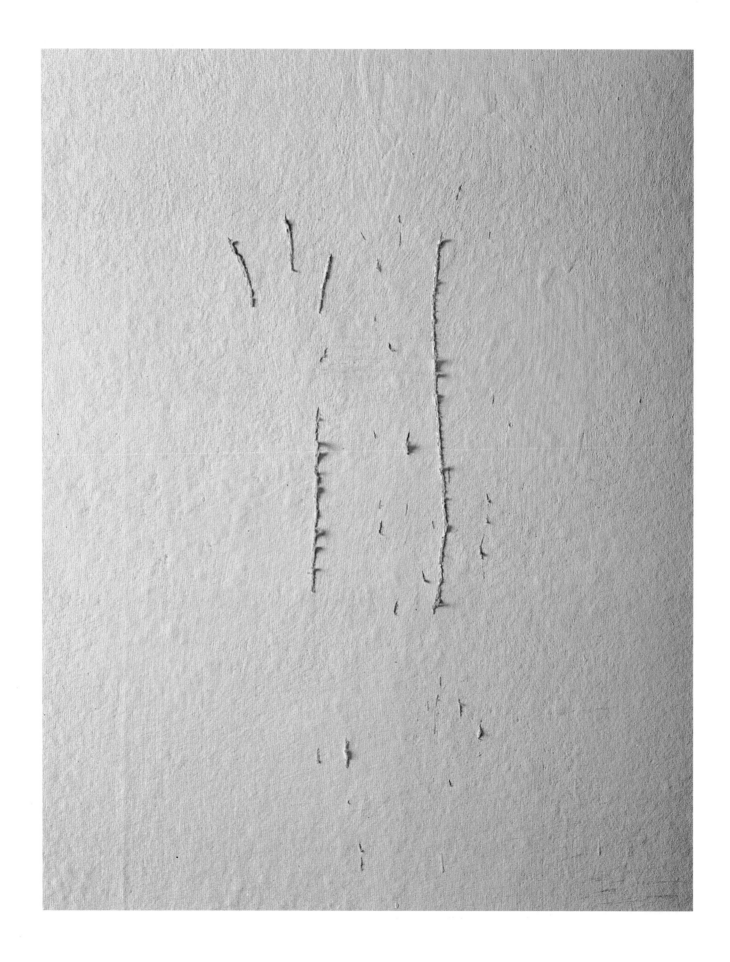

PRINCESS

Elemental Fragmentist

Princess is one of a small number of Elemental Fragmentists, a school of mainly Siamese and Rex painters, whose work is typified by an economy of line and form that conveys only the essential elements of just one part, or fragment, of a subject. This is perhaps the hardest of all feline art to understand and the most difficult to recognize in its formative stages. It was only after Princess had been painting for two years that her owners, Larry and Agnes Martin of Elmhurst, Chicago, realized that all the elements which characterize her present style were apparent in the very first scratches she had made as a kitten on her wooden cat door.

In her more classically minimalist works, Princess uses a set number of angled to vertical strokes (3:2 or 2:3) in a multiplicity of combinations that enable her to explore a wide variety of subjects. We see this clearly in *Amongst the Pigeons* (left), a very early scratching she made on the lounge wall, which has been interpreted as "...perfectly encapsulating the essential

Far left:
Amongst the Pigeons, 1988. Marks with claws on painted fiber-board wall panel, 48 x 72cm. Private collection.

Left:
Princess, (Princess Winklepaw Rothkoko), (b. 1986), will often experiment with sounds during a painting session. The flute mode with a bossa nova beat on this synthesizer is her favorite.

Above:
Princess often works with an upper and lower 'canvas,' using the lower area for preliminary sketch work before proceeding to the final work above. She usually destroys the lower work, but in some cases, prefers it to the upper one which she will claw down instead.

Above right:
Regularly Ridiculed Rodents, 1993. Ink on paper, 52 x 83cm. Patrick Hitchings Collection, Melbourne.
Everything in Princess's work is narrowed to almost totemic simplicity.

elements of the hunted bird's footprints as it makes its final terrified contact with the ground."[1] Other works are not so clear. *Regularly Ridiculed Rodents* (above), for example, has been variously interpreted as depicting two ostracized rats, the essence of cockroach, a functional detail of her paint roller, and, as one would expect, a host of black magic symbols.

Of more interest perhaps, is why she paints these images. Certainly, her art seems to spring simultaneously from prolonged periods of contemplation, periods when she insists on positioning herself in exactly the right place in the room. Does this mean that Princess's elemental forms provide her with the means to plumb the depths and complexities of her own responses to the resonating forces she seems so intent on finding? For although her intention is often unclear, there is a strong suggestion of

[1]*Flavin, Don.* Five Feline Fragmentists. *Exhibition catalog, 1992, Seattle.*

external forces being internalized and translated into a meaningful image.

Does the fact that she is inclined to become sulky and peevish if anything in the room is moved prior to her beginning a painting mean that her deceptively simple structures have to do with complex resonating influences and energy lines that involve ambiguities, paradoxes and tensions arising from the position of movable objects?

Whatever the answers, there can be no doubt that Princess, the cat and the painter, manifests a curiously intense subjectivity, a critical awareness of being both the receiver of energy and its translator. But it is an open subjectivity, a shareable experience. As she rubs up against our legs, purring, at the end of a particularly protracted painting session, we are left in no doubt that her unique interpretations are meant for us too.

Above:
Bounding, 1991. Diluted ink on paper, 64 x 84cm. Museum of Non-Primate Art, Tokyo.
Princess's painting of Boris focuses on the green tag hanging from his collar. The repetition of green dabs and streaks amongst the light brown verticals (which must represent the dog's fur), gives an immediate sense of the tag flicking about as the dog moves, thus capturing the essential nature of canine cavorting.

CHARLIE

Peripheral Realist

Above:
Charlie, (b. 1985), who lives in Sydney, Australia, does all his painting on the refrigerator where the smooth surface allows him to spread the paint quickly and achieve a lively spontaneity.

Right:
The Wild Side, 1991. Acrylic on enamel, 63 x 101cm. Collection of the artist.
Cats use their peripheral vision far more than we realize. This is why they will suddenly look intently in one direction when there seems to us to be nothing there at all. What they are doing of course, is using their more color and movement specific peripheral vision to study objects by looking sideways at them. (You can tell which side by noting the direction of the tail tip —it points in the opposite direction to the side of vision). Charlie has just completed an impressionistic work in which the dishtowel appears as a major motif, and he can be seen checking his subject peripherally.

When Charlie, (Charlie Erwin Schrödinger Jones), was six months old, he was inadvertently shut inside a refrigerator for five hours. Somehow, that event seems to have been a turning point in his life—transforming him virtually overnight into a prolific painter. Many human artists have attributed the sudden urge to express themselves artistically to an emotionally shattering event in their early lives. Both Van Gogh and Picasso suffered pre-pubescent claustrophobic traumas, and it seems possible that Charlie became totally fixated with painting on the refrigerator after being 'punished' by it, in the same way as Picasso's early experience may have been responsible for what Robert Hughes has described as "...the intensity with which he could project his fear of women..."[1] In both cases, their work seems more of an exercise designed to explore, and thereby come to terms with, the object of their disaffection, rather than to celebrate its existence. Of course, their paintings may express a degree of triumphal ascendancy on occasions, but if this suggests celebration, it applies to the successful subjugation of the object rather than to the object itself.

This is not to say that much of Charlie's work fails to consider other objects or states, any more than one would suggest Picasso deals exclusively with subjects that stir his misogynistic tendencies. But we must recognize the fact that, whatever Charlie chooses to paint, he paints it on the refrigerator—the cause of his trauma. One suggestion is that he may simply prefer its smooth surface because it suits his technique, but there are other smooth surfaces, such as the dishwasher and kitchen cupboards to choose from. Another possibility, put forward by psychologist Lyn Ng of the Animal Esthetics Department at Stanford, is that he is marking the refrigerator as a way of asking to be fed. However, Charlie's food is kept in the refrigerator in the cellar, besides which, he meows very loudly when he's hungry.

By painting on the refrigerator, Charlie is most likely doing one of two things. Firstly, he could be trying to change the physical appearance of the original trauma object (which he is forced to live with), thus disguising it and rendering it less powerful, in much the same way as Picasso applied cubist abstractions to female nudes for similar reasons. Alternately, he could be attempting to 'move' the offending trauma object by painting a motif from another part of the room onto it and then, by looking at it peripherally, make it appear to move suddenly in relation to the original position of the motif. Either way, he is able to gain power over it, which must surely be why he paints it.

[1] *Hughes, Robert.* The Shock of the New. *London, Thames & Hudson, 1991.*

BOOTSIE

Trans-Expressionist

Bootsie was neutered, had his tail badly singed by the heater and was sent to a boarding cattery, all in one week at the end of 1989. It was the same week his owners moved house and he was caught (by the dog), attempting to steal the neighbors' half-frozen turkey roast. You'd expect most cats to be subdued by that kind of trauma combination, but not Bootsie. He thrived on it. In fact, it was at the cattery, in Rolling Wood near San Francisco, where they have a creativity program for cats, that he was introduced to painting. Being Bootsie, he took to it at once and has never looked back since. He has had five exhibitions in a little over four years and to date has earned in excess of $75,000.

To watch him paint is pure delight. As soon as the easel is put up on the lawn and the paints are laid out next to it, any hint of feline disdain, any trace of detached hauteur, vanishes completely. He almost pounces on the paint as if he must trap its fleeting vibrance before it escapes, and the moment it is on his paw he springs up to apply it. Consideration appears minimized, while concentration is intense and the strokes are vigorously rhythmical. The process seems to be designed to let body-action fully enter as a composing force, to dictate formal appearances. There is also an obvious intent to lose (loose) self in the work, not holding on to a conscious design, but repeating the strokes as a rhythm, often accompanied by purring which is common among cats who use a high degree of engagement with bodily process while painting. Equally, he may yowl menacingly at the canvas, then suddenly attack it with a quick stroke of paint and spring away as if, in that one decisive action, he had somehow breathed life into an evil force—created a monster that could reach out and grab him by the paw.

The vitality of image that results from this vigorous style can be clearly seen in *Parrot Time* (right). Critic Alfred Auty describes it as "...a poignant expression of nature's inherent dichotomies [where] one is immediately caught up in the primal duality of fight and flight. Red, yellow and blue, slightly angled, slightly curved strokes are laid close together with perfectly controlled flicks of the paw that at once suggest a frenzy of fluttering feathers, leaping upwards, spreading outwards; wing(s) beating—Color! Light! Life! Liberty-within-reach—almost, for now the dominant overlays of negating black which trace the elegant curves of the covetous paw, intrude with dazzling speed to wreak their cruel havoc. Delicate smears of white (fluffy down?), are drawn (ripped) diagonally across the image,

Left:
Bootsie, (b. 1988), uses a vigorous, sometimes aggressive style to explore his inner feelings and perceptions. He won the Zampa d'Oro (Golden Paw) award at the Exposizione dell'Arte Felino in Milan in 1993 and was runner up in 1992.

Above:
Parrot Time, 1992. Acrylic on card, 75 x 72cm. Dr. Philip Wood Collection, Berkeley.

intentionally destroying its integrity and leaving in its place a trembling, all-of-a-twitter confusion. This is a powerful work, for although drawn in by a strong narrative factor, we are nevertheless denied a final dénouement, and so left feeling uneasy and perplexed."[1]

In a recent interview, Bootsie's owner described him as "...liking to leap about and put different colors all over the place without much caring how he does it." However, Auty feels that "...this seemingly carefree 'non-serious' method conceals a deeper concern. It is not the content of life which he paints," he explains, "but the experiential feel of its rhythm. The feel for instance of the unique energy at the point of harmonic resonance; of its intensity registered all-at-once, pre-edited, as a perfect liaison of kinetic forces which derive from the slightest of actions, the most minimal of thoughts."[2]

Bootsie's method of achieving this integration is flamboyant and full of an idiosyncratic concern that typifies many of his recent works. The confrontational blacks of *Parrot Time,* for example, are echoed in his well-known *Cocking for Cockatoos* (right), in which a long-nosed green dog

Below:
Bootsie in full flight during painting of *Hands Up! Mr. Rooster,* which sold for $15,000. Note the rough sketch he made for this work on the back of the canvas.

attempts to urinate (yellow), on a small flock of low-flying cockatoos (white). The inner message in *Parrot Time* is perhaps more obvious, but *Cocking for Cockatoos,* with its clever suggestion of canine incompetence, gains rather than loses by not being overly pedantic.

Bootsie refuses to be trapped in a recognizable style, but the strong physicality of gesture which tended to dominate (and perhaps limit) his earlier work is increasingly replaced by more tangible and delicately controlled marks that help to soften and add meaning to his less subtle gestures. This must enable him to explore his feelings and perceptions in greater detail and so arrive at a more satisfying understanding of his own unique place in the world.

[1]*Auty, A.* The Feline Procrustean Ethic in Trans-Expressionism. *Paper delivered to the annual conference of the centre de recherche dans les arts graphiques félins, Paris, 1993.* [2] *ibid.*

Above:
Cocking for Cockatoos, 1993. Acrylic on card and plaster board, 110 x 95cm. Scraatchi Collection, London. Bootsie's painting has a refreshing rawness which enables the viewer to experience the physicality of the artist's deep relationship with process.

RUSTY

Psychometric Impressionist

Psychometric Impressionism involves the creation of images which reflect, not the appearance of a particular object, but rather the situations or locations the object has been involved with in the past. In order to create such a work, the cat will spend a good deal of time sniffing, patting and rubbing against the object or animal whose psychometric impression it wants to convey, before it commences its painting. Because of their psychic abilities, cats are highly adept at this form of expression and Rusty, an Abyssinian who hails from Edinburgh, along with Muscat in Paris, is one of the world's leading exponents of the art. Like Muscat, he is highly sensitive to small changes in static electricity and therefore something of a premonitionist, often being

able to accurately predict certain events before they occur.

Rusty's choice of subject matter seems to be contingent upon whether it has some special significance for him, though this is not the aspect he expresses in his paintings. In *Blue Bike Blues* for example (page 76), he chose a bicycle that a child had used to deliberately run over his tail the day before. However, it is not the bike nor this event which he explores in the work, but rather an incident which occurred while he was away and his owner tripped over the bike when carrying two large bags of bottled beer. In the ensuing furor, the bike was hurled onto the neighbors' roof where it unfortunately became entangled with their TV antenna. If they (the Australian neighbors), had not been watching a live telecast of the cricket from Sydney at the time the painting may never have happened. Certainly, the bike wouldn't have ended up impaled on top of his iron gate where Rusty couldn't fail to notice it on his return home from the vet. But whether or not this prompted him to paint it, the remarkable thing is that even though he never saw the bike on the antenna, he not only rubbed himself against the bike, but also spent a good hour rubbing against the neighbours' antenna before he began to paint.

Chapter
4 | Other Forms of Artistic Expression

The number of domestic cats actively painting in the world today is minuscule, maybe a few hundred at the very most out of the estimated two hundred million currently living with human beings. There are, however, many more hundreds of cats who use other forms of artistic expression and no survey of this kind would be complete without some reference to them.

A few cats continue to use types of process art such as sculpture or scratch-forms in addition to their painting, but for the majority, the various non-painting techniques usually represent the first stage of their artistic growth and cease to be developed once painting has become firmly established. It is true that some cats begin to paint with little or no preliminary exploration of these more rudimentary forms but, for most, they represent the essential initiating element and are of great significance in determining the future direction of their creativity. Indeed, it is by examining these initial efforts that we are able to gain not only an understanding of the genesis of the primal feline aesthetic gesture but, by inference, possibly move closer to an appreciation of our own artistic beginnings.

Left:
Maxwell with *Gerty*, a work in progress. Clever use of negative space between the loosened brocade and its upper support seems to imply an open mouth, while his intricate claw work on the adjacent apex gives a subtle indication of wet nose catching the light. Two vertical threads hanging from the lower jaw now immediately suggest drooling and the whole work (including the legs) almost certainly portrays the frontal aspect of Gertrude, the St. Bernard with whom Maxwell shares his home.

Right:
Interpretive diagram by R.A. Scull, 1993.

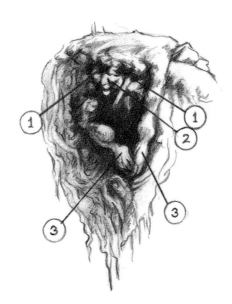

Above:
Strontium with *Passing Through*, 1990. Appropriated couch, 56 x 33 x 42cm. H.Busch Collection, New Zealand. One interpretation (diagram left), suggests a facial form is developed as the predominant territorial sign: (1) eyes, (2) nose, (3) front legs.

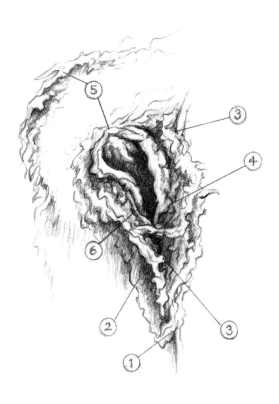

Above:
Constructional diagram by Anne Hindry.
The numbers refer to the amount of time
(in weeks) taken over each section.

Above right:
Oedipus, *Opening*, 1992. Appropriated
red couch, 68 x 37 x 29cm. Collection of
the artist. When this piece was first shown
in The Los Angeles Exhibition of Feline
Process Art, in 1993, it received great
praise from Gertrude Greer who saw it as
"...a very exciting, obviously invertist
work...certainly more powerful than his
later painted images with their rather
boring predominance of phallocentric
verticals."

The widespread domestic use of upholstered furniture from the turn of
the century on, has had a profound effect on the development of a feline
aesthetic. Unlike loose materials such as curtains, tablecloths and the like,
the fabric covering furniture is stretched firmly over padding and held in
place by wooden supports which enables it to be progressively degraded in
a controlled manner over a long period of time.

A cat making a territorial mark on a tree trunk leaves scratch marks
which, with repeated marking, become deeper and bolder rather than
more complex. However, the cat, marking on upholstery very quickly
sees its initial sign changing as progressive scratching degrades the integrity
of the fibers. Egon Lübel, writing in *The Biology of Feline Art*, describes
what happens next. "Now its thin vertical mark has become something

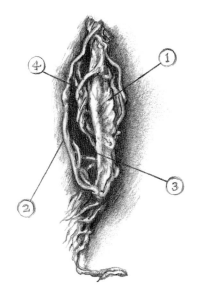

Above:
Bonny, *Come On In*, 1990. Appropriated lounge chair, 92 x 89 x 78cm. Private collection.

Above:
Clyde interacts with his sister's sculpture, allowing his whole body to become implicated in its heavily nuanced form.

Above:
Interpretive diagram by Peter Muxlow:
1. Tail form.
2. Erogenous edging.
3. Ovoidal aperture.
4. Restrictive vine forms.
"The synthetic fiber has been carefully frayed to resemble the texture and color of a cat's tail in the upright welcoming position—inviting, yet guarding the entrance beyond. However, this controlling tail is itself compromised by restrictive vines so that the whole erogenously edged aperture hints at pleasure tinged with the possibility of entanglement."
Muxlow, M. *Clawstraphobias*. Exhibition catalog, Drexel Gallery of Non-Primate Art, Philadelphia, 1992.

else—a hole, a shredded slit, or maybe a bulbous profusion of foam. For some cats, a point comes when it accepts this new construction as its own mark and, using its innate ability to copy, attempts to repeat it. This is the very beginning of representational art—the dawning of an artistic sensibility. Then, in the process of trying to replicate [its new mark], another begins to emerge from the increasingly tattered fabric, and now our copying cat must make a decision; which will it duplicate? Which does it prefer? This is the moment of its first truly intentional aesthetic gesture."

Although the techniques used in these upholstery works may look simple enough, the older, less flexible fabrics and coarse horsehair stuffings involve considerable modelling problems and some cats have to resort to binding fibers together excrementally, or add the required textural interest with salivary deposits. Owing almost entirely to owner ignorance, many cats are not given access to paints at this stage and forced to continue with soft sculpture. For them, the increasing use of furniture made of easily worked synthetic materials and simply degradable, yet coherent foams, has, on the surface, been beneficial. But these modern mediums are not without their problems and it is now becoming progressively difficult to distinguish between serious attempts to develop new signs which make full use of the feline aesthetic and what Lübel describes as "the merely dilettantish reliance on the occasional dramatic effect."

However, much of this upholstery work is not without merit and a recent eagerness by cat artists to find sculptural equivalents for feline experience has seen the construction of elegant works which draw their

audience (other cats) into the work by actual physical participation.

Of course, transmutable media like upholstery are not crucial to the development of a cat's creative ability. Marking on a dense substance like wood, provided it is done over a long period and in compliance with the two natural laws which govern effective territorial signing, can also initiate an aesthetic sense. To be powerful, a territorial mark must first be repeated as often as possible in the most highly populated areas so it becomes widely known amongst a given population of cats. Secondly, it must be distinctive, yet still easily recognizable as a territorial demarcation. A cat using such a mark in this way will be rewarded with a well-secured territory. Each time it makes its special mark, each time it sees it, the cat feels secure and is encouraged to repeat the process. Gradually, the artist becomes better at it, is able to do it more quickly and learns where it is most effective. Eventually, this evolving aesthetic judgement and technical skill may develop into the ability to make representational marks.

This seems to have been the way in which Angel, a ten-year-old American Havana Brown who lives in Kilcullen near Dublin, slowly realized her ability to make imitative scratchings. *How Now?* (left) scratched on a round wooden gate post is typical of her considered Land Art style. Inspiration is almost always another living thing, in this case Isabella the Jersey cow, but she has also completed separate invertist scratchings on a motor mower, a sheep's skull and a discarded white plastic potty, *Bottoms Up,* 1991. Her relationship with Isabella spans her entire life. As a kitten, she delighted in jumping at the cow's swishing tail and later found the floppish quality of the lightly patted teat irresistible. Inevitably, she uncovered the secret of milk, but before she could work out exactly how to take advantage of it, Isabella sat on her. For nearly a minute, the whole of Angel's little body was completely enveloped in the warm rubbery folds of Isabella's stifling udder.

This experience was profoundly formative for the young artist. The resulting relationship with Isabella is obvious in many of her recent scratchings such as *How Now?* and *Over the Moon,* but the lack of trust it engendered finds expression in her approach to many other subjects, too. In a work clearly intended to depict the neighboring Alsatian-Collie cross, for example, she carefully shredded the front of a cane chair to almost perfectly replicate a side view of its long fur. When, after six months, the work was finally completed to her satisfaction, she urinated all over it and never touched it again.

While aesthetic clawing is a relatively common feline creative technique, one must be careful to distinguish between the irrelevant and destructive scratchings that are occasionally exhibited by ignorant owners in the hope of financial gain, and those scratch-forms which demonstrate a high degree of considered artistic intent. There can be little doubt of this

Above:
Ever since the udder incident, Angel's relationship with Isabella, the cow, has been tinged with a degree of revenge. Each day Isabella must pass through several gates on her way to and from milking. Angel takes this opportunity to jump onto her back and explore the finer textural details of her bony hide. This infuriates Isabella who tries everything, including a kind of bovine hypnosis, to stop her.

Left:
How Now? 1993. Scratched gate post, 151 x 28 x 28cm. Owner's collection. Angel's feelings towards Isabella are clearly stated in this recent work. "The post itself seems representative of both cow and relationship. Encircling wires bite deep into the wood, subtly bulging it out like an abundant udder, while deep vertical fissures spoil the surface and threaten its integrity. The claw marks, with additional cow dung to add contrast, are drawn at an oblique angle in four distinct groupings, which when viewed as the four corners of a three-dimensional box, equate with the four hanging teats of the udder. Now the deep gouging scratches, which may have previously been considered over worked, take on a new significance." (Exhib. Catg.)

Far right:
Bad Cat, 1991. Appropriated venetian blinds, 114 x 167cm. Rosemarie Trickel Trust, Berkeley. It required nine months of diligent gnawing and clawing to create this bold image of a cat searing its way through a domestic techno-barrier. The work clearly alludes to the constraining effect of mass-produced products on the contemporary cat's freedom of movement.

Below:
Fritz with *When the Cat's Away,* 1990. Claw marks on painted metal, 16 x 67cm. photo courtesy of The Institute for the Promotion of Cat Art, London.

when the work has taken a long time to complete, especially in the case of a chewing or mouth sculpture, which is usually the product of great dedication by a cat with a determined sense of purpose. *Bad Cat* (right), by Fritz (Fritz de Flayed-Mouse Fischl) of Los Angeles, falls into this category.

What immediately strikes the eye is the bold use of negative space to create the image of a cat (tail upright, front leg forward) walking straight towards us—striding defiantly through this mean, light-slitting, mass produced techno-barrier that curls back as if melted by searing heat. Fritz is not swayed by any promptings of feline Zeitgeist and while his work arguably borders on the Avant-Grunge with its celebration of second-degree white trash, it nevertheless brings into focus the artist's serious concern with the confining effects of modern technology on the domestic cat. Fritz's death in 1993 (electrocuted while completing a reconstructionist sculpture on a TV cord), was a great loss to the movement, but he leaves behind an impressive œuvre including his well known Barbie chewings, *The Zen of Ken*, 1991, and *The Sound of One Leg Flapping*, 1992.

Cats possess an exceptionally flexible skeletal structure and a well muscled body which enables them to adopt and hold a large repertoire of poses for long periods of time. Despite this, surprisingly few choose body sculpture as a mode of artistic expression. The few cat owners who insist otherwise often fail to distinguish between their cat's rehearsal of the extremely slow, controlled movements necessary for hunting by stealth and genuine examples of performance art which involve frozen body positions specifically designed to effect a change in the viewer. These performances are usually put on for the benefit of other cats and, although they may occasionally display for mice and even birds, they seldom bother

Left:
By mimicking the pointy and whiskered nature of a mouse's nose, this cat is able to impress her viewer with an impassioned characterization of the victim position.

Below:
Misty uses her own body to make a living sculpture of a mouse, thereby creating an empathetic, one-to-one communication between artist and viewer, cat and mouse.

with dogs, who for some reason become highly agitated and often aggressive when viewing this form of art.

Accentuation is a type of aesthetic expression which can present difficulties in interpretation because of its similarity to advanced territorial marking techniques. Unlike the various scratch-forms which create new images by degrading and reforming an appropriated article, accentuation is a kind of decoration which involves the application of a medium to another object or artwork in order to enhance or accentuate some aspect of it. There is no easy method of distinguishing between gestures of accentuation and signs made to denote ownership but, generally speaking, the former are a good deal more complex than territorial marks need to be. A real problem emerges, however, where two cats decide to engage in competitive marking, each one adding a mark to counter the other's until the object is covered with an often intricately impastoed effect. In such cases it is crucial to have actually witnessed the painting process in order to ascertain whether or not it constitutes a valuable work of accentuation.

Above:
Merry Fishmess, 1989. Acrylic on wooden fish, 72 x 39 x 37cm. Private collection.

The status of these two artists is enough to confirm that this adornment of a wooden fish constitutes a genuine work of decorative accentuation rather than being the end product of a competitive territorial marking session. Julie (right) is well known for her clever accentuating daubings on obsolete Italian nautical charts and Schnabley Puss, for his striking mixed media metamorphoses involving fish paste and turkey bones on broken milk saucers.

Above:
The cat's ability to draw clear lines to accentuate the territorial position of its feces is constrained by unsuitable marking media such as coarse litter (page 27).

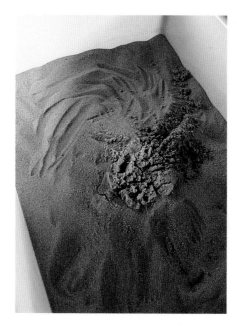

Cats with access to fine damp sand are better able to produce a multiplicity of well-demarcated grooves and interesting textural effects which are more likely to stimulate the development of an aesthetic response.

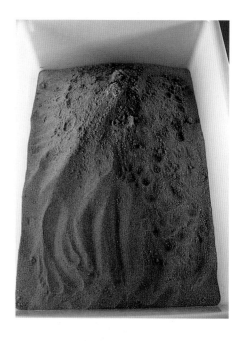

The classic litter-tray pattern involves two or three deep grooves arrowing towards the feces. Obsessive marking by insecure cats often results in their creating new curved lines to accentuate their deposits.

Above:
A simple, somewhat overworked curvilinear design with the beginnings of a second curve which traces the first, and shows an incipient ability to copy.

Above:
A more complex pattern of finely executed curves which effectively incorporates the bottom of the litter tray into the overall fluidity of design.

Above:
A very advanced, swirling (possibly tail symbolist), motif with interesting (w)hole effects. A well-balanced composition—the work of a creatively advanced cat.

91

Above:
Fluff, *Untitled*, work in progress, 1994.
Playing with paints in the bathroom often
leads on to serious paintings like this.

Above:

Many cats play with wool but Fluff uses it to construct creative installations. Her technique has developed rapidly over three years and as her owner notes, "She uses less wool but more colors than she used to and now she makes really tight knots and goes all over the place with it." These remarks are substantiated by critic Christine Carswell who reviewed the work in *Cat Art Today*. "Fluff demonstrates a greater precision of detail and economy of means than in her formative installations. The strongly accented and tightly (cruelly?) tangled nodes of intensity are finer, while color and shape have a less formal coherence which contributes to the eloquence of these shapes that are highly suggestive of deceased, or nearly deceased, prey. The disturbing presence of these ephemeral constructions intrude into her living space and suggest an imposed sense of ceremony which has been an integral feature of many of Fluff's works. If excitement, rapture and delectability are woven into the texture of this installation, I also read a cleansing, a washing away of the hunter's guilt that goes far beyond any complacent paw licking."

Left:
Fluff, *Prey Presto!* 1993. Installation, wool on carpet, 149 x 93cm.

Above:
Radar prepares a mouse for one of his nocturnal installations. These sometimes involve the use of stairs to create interesting spatial juxtapositions.

Installations involving dead animals or parts of dead animals have had an unfortunate history of misunderstanding. The human intolerance of rodents in particular, and a revulsion of unskinned or unplucked animal bodies in general, has resulted in the destruction of many valuable feline works using these forms. Worse still, the numerous cats who choose to express themselves by carefully displaying these 'tokens of life' in the home, where they can best be appreciated and protected, are admonished for their efforts and, as a result, discouraged from pursuing the only line of creative endeavor they know.

By bringing dead, or nearly dead prey back to the center of their territory, many cats are simply making a reciprocal gesture—leaving freshly killed food in return for the food they have been given by their owners. However, there are a growing number of cats, both male and female, who reportedly go to great pains to arrange and rearrange these small carcasses

or sections of carcass, with so much care and precision over such a long period of time, that the resulting designs can be none other than well-considered forms of artistic expression.

Radar, a seven-year-old Black-tipped British Shorthair female who lives in Santa Monica, has benefited greatly as a result of her owners' enlightened encouragement. Over the last three years, they have compiled an impressive photographic record of all her works, including a video (that she never tires of watching) of a kinetic installation in which a wingless dragonfly interacts with an almost lifeless shrew—a disturbingly poignant work that at times boarders on the profane. Unlike other well-known 'live' installationists who also use inanimate objects—Bully in Seoul (knitting needles and fish), or Moro in Milan (cardboard dolls and snails), Radar works exclusively with animate, or once-animate, objects. Her installations are meticulously constructed over a period of days, each piece being delicately patted into a variety of revealing positions until the relationship between all the elements has been thoroughly explored.

Reviewing a photographic exhibition of Radar's installations, critic John Ribberts wrote, "Of all her works, I was most deeply touched by the least complex, *Infra-mice* (left), a beautifully balanced and peaceful arrangement of two dead mice who seem to float together on a calm gray ocean. Their tiny bodies, wet and dishevelled, merge together as if swept along by some powerful force, yet only their heads join—a union of spiritual intent, a brief harmony of vision that is made all the more painfully real by the wide gulf that opens between their bodies and long flowing tails. Radar shows a fascination here with the inevitability of separation and the corresponding need to struggle for contact. The problem is how to achieve this without surrendering that deep sense of feline independence the artist must feel in her innermost being."

Left:
Radar, *Infra-mice*, 1994. Temporary installation, lounge carpet, 13 x 12cm. Santa Monica. Thanks to her owners' enlightened encouragement, Radar's meticulous constructions with 'stabilized' life forms now show a great maturity and clear sense of purpose.

ACKNOWLEDGEMENTS

Planning, research, writing and photography for this book have taken the best part of seven years to complete. We are deeply indebted to the many people who have given so generously of their time and knowledge during this period.

Our special thanks go to the numerous cat owners and members of cat art societies all over the world who gave us access to their photographic records and allowed us to observe and photograph their cats at work. In particular we would like to mention; Lynda Aitken, Mrs. Andersen, Val & Kevin Ball, Robert & Michelle Barge, Bob Barge, Liz Beasley, Anna Bell, Gael Binns, Jacqui & William Bonne, Sue Bradley, Rose & Fred Brittain, Beverley Brown, Dawn & Donna Burgess, Polly Buring, Mrs. & Lynda Coogan, Bill, Arja & Bran Davis, Lyn Davis, Sofia di Baci, Mrs. Chris Franklin, Margaret Gough, Sheldon Gunn, Gwenyth & John Halson, Jo & Murray Hedges, Hilma Hultenburg, Lorraine Kef, Edith Kern, Miri King, Berryl Lewis, Sandee Lidbetter, Nora Mann, Larry & Agnes Martin, Colin McCahon, Pam Nathan, Alli, Clive & Phyll Payton, Ginny Rastall, Maizy Reece, Margaret & John Ridge, Denise & Guy Sandle, Lorna & Don Simpson, Mrs. Stein, Jane Standenburg, & Ellie Taylor.

In particular, we wish to acknowledge the assistance we received from the Iris Mary Davies Memorial Trust, without whose generous contribution this book would not have been possible. Iris Mary Davies was the first person to suggest that human thought may be the crucial trigger in stimulating cats to begin marking with paint. Her clear, uncomplicated observations pre-dated the first scientific publication of the theory of inter-species morphic resonance by more than five years.

In a letter to a friend in 1976 she wrote,

.....so once I'd sent you Tiger's paintings and you'd seen them for yourself, you knew for sure that cats could paint. Now maybe that knowledge, that certainty that some cats can paint, created a type of positive force that started your lovely Blackie off doing it too. You see, I think it has to be something more than some energy field created by my cat doing something new here, that somehow made your cat, sixty miles away, all at once start doing the same thing. If it was like those monkeys you mentioned that suddenly started to wash their potatoes just after other monkeys on another island learned to do it, then why did it take Blackie two years to start painting? Why did he begin just after I posted you Tiger's pictures and why hadn't a cat around here begun to paint too? I'm convinced it was your knowing the possibility of cats painting, created an energy that was a kind of starter for your cat. Like water for a seed that's been dormant in the desert for years.

It is hoped that the wealth of feline creativity contained in these pages will stand as a tribute to Iris Mary Davies, and go some way in furthering her vision of a world in which animals are truly our partners.

SELECTED BIBLIOGRAPHY

In addition to articles and books noted in the text, this list contains both titles of a general nature and more academic works for those who wish to read in detail about particular topics mentioned in this volume.

ARK, P. 1992. **Copy Cats**. *Evidence of Representational Invertism in Feline Territorial Demarcation Activity*. Varnadoe & Kirk, NY.

ARORA, D. **Psychedelicacy**. The Effects of Catmint on the Creative Behaviour of Domestic Cats on Long Island. *Cat Art Today*, Vol. II 1992.

BALL, H. 1992. **Paws for Thought**. *The Magic & Meaning of Litter Tray Relief Patterns*. Slive & Seymour, Cambridge.

BORG. G. 1982. **The Bark Scratchings of Northern Australia**. McMahon University Press, Darwin, 1990.

CIACOMETTI, A. 1989. **Forget the Cat, Save The Art**. *A Reappraisal*. Raspail Schwitters & Prat, Lyon.

COVERT, J. **Alley Art**. *Bad Cats Do Their Stuff*. Dryfhout Press, New Hampshire.

DENIS, M. 1989. **More Paw Less Claw**. *Helping Your Cat Develop a Better Technique*. Order Press, New York.

FOGLE, B. 1991. **The Cat's Mind**. Pelham Books, London.

HERGOTT, E. (Ed.), 1993. **The Cat Artists Index**. *A Biographical Index of American Painters & Scratchers*. Flex Books, Boston.

LARSEN, K. 1987. **Understanding Art Writing.** *A Reader's Dictionary*. Kimmelman Reference Library, New York.

LONG, R. 1990. **Feline Artistic Potential**. *Stretching Your Cat Creatively*. Knight & Christopher, Los Angeles.

LORD-OSIS, J. **Pawnography**. Paw marking as a mode of sexual communication amongst domestic cats in Sweden. *Journal of Applied Aesthetics,* Vol. VI, 1991.

LUKAX, A. 1987 **Felineistine**. *Destructivism & the New Feline Aesthetic*. Pagan Books, Boston.

LUXE, C. **Matisse at Beaurivage**. A dissertation on exact easel positioning as it relates to possible points of harmonic reasonance. *New Cat Art*, Vol. III, 1992.

MARANDEL, J. 1986. **Pawtrayals & Pawtents**. *Cat Marks and Their Secret Meanings*. Crystal Arts, Berkeley.

MORRIS, P. 1962. **The Language of the Tail**. Fulica Press, Ascot.

MUTT, R. **Decorative Retromingency**. Urinary embellishment as a major problem in the curation of feline art. *Journal of Non-Primate Art*, Vol. XV, 1991.

PALETTIE, P. 1983. **Cross-Breeds, Criticism & Curation**. *A Complete Guide to Cat Painting*. Buhler & Lynes, Baltimore.

ROSENBLOOM, R. 1990. **Persian Art & Craft**. Bothmer & Bernard, New York.

SIVINTY, L.N.& P.T. 1972. **Udjat Cat**. *An Epistemology of Cat Marking in Ancient Egypt*. Umbawarrah University Press, Perth.

TANCOCK, J. 1988. **La vie et l'œuvre de Minnie Monet Manet**. Rosenberg & Schnapper, Paris.

WUNDERLICH, R. 1993. **Why Dogs Don't Paint**. Da Costa & Kaufmann, Princeton.

1 9 8 0

1 9 8 1

1 9 8 2

Edward Lucie-Smith

1 9 8 3

A R T   I N   T H E   E I G H T I E S

1 9 8 4

1 9 8 5

1 9 8 6

1 9 8 7

1 9 8 8

PHAIDON · OXFORD
PHAIDON UNIVERSE · NEW YORK

1 9 8 9

To Susan and Robert Summer

Published in Great Britain by Phaidon Press Limited, Musterlin House, Jordan
Hill Road, Oxford OX2 8DP

ISBN 0 7148 2609 X Hb
ISBN 0 7148 2610 3 Pb

A CIP catalogue record for this book is available from the British Library

Published in the United States of America by Phaidon Universe, 381 Park
Avenue South, New York, N.Y. 10016

ISBN 0-87663-600-8

A CIP catalog record for this book is available from the Library of Congress

First published 1990
© Phaidon Press Limited 1990
Text © Edward Lucie-Smith 1990

Book design by James Campus

Phototypeset by Tradespools Ltd., Frome, Somerset
in Linotype Garamond 3
Printed in Spain by H. Fournier SA, Vitoria

CONTENTS

Mimmo Paladino. *Noa Noa*. **1983. Oil on panel,**
53 × 40 cm (21 × 15³/₄ in). Private Collection

INTRODUCTION: THE NEW SPIRIT IN PAINTING

On 15 January 1981 the Royal Academy of Arts in London, not hitherto noted for its whole-hearted support of the avant-garde, and situated in a country where the critics and exhibition-going public were both still slightly suspicious of modernism, a new show opened entitled *A New Spirit in Painting*. The exhibition was an attempt to predict what would seem artistically important during the decade to follow. Like all such attempts, it was only partially successful. Nevertheless, its inclusions and omissions were highly significant for the art of the 1980s.

The first thing to notice about *A New Spirit in Painting* is the emphasis on 'painting'. During the 1970s it had often seemed as if the traditional distinction between painting and sculpture was about to be abolished. Art 'at the cutting edge' (I think this phrase was already current) paid little heed to whether work was two-dimensional or three-dimensional. When they were completely free to make a choice, artists almost instinctively opted for the greater freedom of three-dimensionality – and also for what they felt to be the greater honesty of work from which any pretence at creating an illusion had been banished. Where the re-creation or reconstruction of three-dimensional appearances upon a flat surface actually occurred, it tended to be regarded with suspicion. The exhibition at the Royal Academy asserted that the separation between the genres continued to be a valid one, and that there were indeed things which a painter could accomplish and which a sculptor could not do.

An analysis of the actual contents of the show yields information of great interest. Thirty-eight artists were included. Some had been major stars for a long time – Francis Bacon, David Hockney, Willem de Kooning, Matta, Pablo Picasso, Frank Stella, Andy Warhol. Some were senior figurative artists who up to this point had seemed a little isolated from what post-war modernism was really about – Balthus and Lucian Freud. Some were Minimalists, practitioners of one of the best-established art styles of the late 1960s and 1970s – these included Alan Charlton (British), Gotthard Graubner (German), Brice Marden and Robert Ryman (both American). There were also members of the *Arte Povera* group which had flourished in Italy during the same period – Pier Paolo Calzolari, Jannis Kounellis, Mario Merz.

Markus Lüpertz. *Occupier: Midday (Das Collier des Siegers)*. 1983. Oil on linen, 165 × 133 cm (65 × 52¹/₂ in). Courtesy Mary Boone Gallery, New York

There were also a number of inclusions which helped to give *A New Spirit in Painting* a novel and revolutionary tone. In the first place, there was a large group of German artists, whose work was loosely related to the old German Expressionism of the pre-World War I and Weimar years – Georg Baselitz, Rainer Fetting, K.H. Hödicke, Anselm Kiefer, Bernd Koberling, Markus Lüpertz, A.R. Penck, Sigmar Polke. Most of these artists were already much exhibited in Germany itself, but for the majority the Royal Academy exhibition marked their international breakthrough. More than half had not exhibited on such an acknowledged level previously – that is, with the likes of Bacon, de Kooning, Stella and Warhol. To this group of Germans were added artists of other nationalities whose work looked a little like theirs. Among them were Sandro Chia and Mimmo Paladino (Italian), and Julian Schnabel (American). For most critics, these inclusions were the most important aspect of the show.

Jannis Kounellis. *Installation at Walcot Chapel, Bath.*
Artsite Gallery, Bath Festival Exhibition 1987

Roberto Marquez. *Mirrors Have No Mercy*. 1988. Oil on canvas,
152 × 183 cm (60 × 72 in). Courtesy Riva Yares Gallery, Scottsdale Arizona

The excitement generated by the emergence of the German Neo-Expressionist school and its allies was so intense that few people realized that *A New Spirit in Painting* had also drastically rearranged the established hierarchies of British modernism. The show abruptly discarded the opposition between the British versions of Pop Art and of Post-Painterly Abstraction (work by members of the Situation Group, founded at the beginning of the 1960s), in favour of a new 'School of London' – the phrase had been coined in 1976 by the British-domiciled American, R.B. Kitaj. The School of London spanned several generations. It removed Bacon and Freud from their hitherto isolated situations, and put them at the head of a motley band which included Frank Auerbach, Kitaj himself and Howard Hodgkin. Later Leon Kossoff and Michael Andrews were to be proposed as additional members.

Despite the inclusion of a number of major artists from America, it is clear that the exhibition organizers believed that the creative energy was now more likely to be found elsewhere. Only nine Americans were included, two of them (Kitaj and Cy Twombly) permanently domiciled in Europe, whereas there were no fewer than eleven Germans. Within Europe, the emphasis was heavily on Nordic countries. There were only two Frenchmen (Balthus and Jean Hélion), plus a Frenchman-by-courtesy, Pablo Picasso, who in any case was no longer alive. Set against the general development of post-war modernism,

from Abstract Expressionism onwards, all this marked a radical change of direction. New York was no longer the force it had been; the old Ecole de Paris, which had survived into the 1950s, was quite definitively dead.

I have analysed the contents of *A New Spirit in Painting* in detail because the exhibition accurately prophesied the direction the visual arts would take in the course of the decade that followed. Some of its prophecies were self-fulfilling – they were bound to come about once they had been made. The controversy aroused by the decision to include so many new German artists propelled the whole German school into the limelight. German Neo-Expressionist artists became major international stars, at a level reserved during the previous three decades for the major artists of the school of New York and for almost no others.

It was agreed in many quarters that the creative initiative had indeed returned to Europe. It was not merely European artists, but also European critics, curators and museum directors who began to show a new independence. During the post-war epoch an exhibition circuit had been created in Europe, which had been one of

the chief means of disseminating the message of American art. It included a number of important German museums, plus the Stedelijk Museum in Amsterdam, the Kunsthalle in Basel, Modernamuseet in Stockholm and the Louisiana Museum in Denmark. All of these institutions began to show increased interest in what was happening on their own doorsteps – the emphasis was, once again, on northern rather than southern European artists. France suffered from a lack of forceful and convincing new talents, with the result that the Centre Pompidou in Paris pursued a policy which was oriented towards survey shows of the earlier years of modernism – the period when Paris had, indeed, been the centre of the art world. In Italy there were many new artists and new art movements but no major institution which regularly staged avant-garde exhibitions. The Venice Biennale, with its chronic lack of focus, was not an acceptable sub-

Frank Auerbach. *Primrose Hill, Early Summer*. 1982. Oil on board, 40 × 50 cm (15³/₄ × 19³/₄ in). Courtesy Marlborough Fine Art

stitute. The gap was only filled towards the end of the 1980s, by the creation of a new exhibition centre at Palazzo Grassi in Venice and a new Museum of Modern Art at Prato. Showings of avant-garde art in London, divided between the Tate Gallery, the Royal Academy and the Hayward Gallery (the last under the direction of the Arts Council of Great Britain and then of its successor,

the South Bank Arts Board), continued to be somewhat erratic, but there was a provincial exhibition circuit of growing ambition and interest.

If *A New Spirit in Painting* openly promoted the cause of the new German art, it also put forward other significant ideas, at least by implication. Both the choice of German artists and the choice of British ones suggested that the age of modernist internationalism was coming to an end. All of the German Neo-Expressionists were deeply concerned with the idea of what it was to be German. They tackled German traumas and explored German cultural roots. The British exhibitors were not as consciously and vehemently nationalist, but the choice of painters and paintings seemed to suggest that there was a growing preoccupation with specifically British qualities. British Pop (entirely absent apart from David Hockney, who showed work which had very little connection with the Pop movement) had, on the contrary, tended to stress the many links between British and American mass culture, and the homogeneous character of industrial society taken as a whole.

Even more significant was the pluralism of the show. The things which the Minimalists tried to communicate were so different from those which preoccupied the figurative painters shown side by side with them that it seemed as if a completely different critical language was required to assess their work. All pretence vanished that contemporary art possessed intellectual unity however different the guises in which it presented itself. More importantly, *A New Spirit in Painting* undermined the theory that modernism in the post-World War II epoch had consisted of a dialectic of styles, with each new movement taking up and then either enlarging upon or refuting the arguments put forward by its immediate predecessor. Here were works of art made at the same point in time, and hung, as it now happened, in the same building, but with essentially nothing to say to one another.

One of the ways in which the artistic climate has changed most markedly since the exhibition is in the huge and sudden expansion of the universe of contemporary art. Since 1981 there has been a plethora of exhibitions devoted to Latin American art, and an almost equal plethora devoted to art from the Soviet Union. Both of these phenomena put the Western European or North American critic into difficulties. Latin America has been producing modernist painting and sculpture since the beginning of the 1920s. But this activity was for a long time overshadowed by the Muralist movement in Mexico, which borrowed certain ideas from early modernism without itself being fully modern. One of the chief things it retained from the nineteenth century was the notion that the artist could not be part of an elite but must be a fully participating member of a mass society. The Russian Constructivists also professed this ideal; but it was figurative Mexican artists such as Diego Rivera and José Clemente Orozco who came much closer to fulfilling it.

The prolonged success of the Muralist movement planted the idea that Latin American art was essentially the product of a mixed, non-European culture, and a retort to European colonialism. This is an explanation which partially fits the facts in Mexico, the cradle of Muralism, but which is utterly implausible when applied to the art of countries such as Chile or Argentina, or even Venezuela. It cannot be denied that art plays an important public role in Latin American culture, and that the Latin American element is increasingly making itself felt as a real presence in the United States, where it has become symbolic of the emergence of a new, distinctively Hispanic culture. But European and North American interpretations of the Latin American art of today too frequently try to force it into a mould which was broken when Muralism died in the 1960s.

If there is one theme which seems to be important in the Latin American art of the 1980s, it is the emergence of a form of 'magic realism' which is equivalent to the strange mingling of realism and fantasy in the work of the

Jacobo Borges. *A.* 1988. Oil on canvas, 168.5 × 142 cm (66¹/₄ × 56³/₄ in). cm (Courtesy CDS Gallery, New York

novelist Gabriel Garcia Marquez. This dream-like, yet totally veracious quality can be found in the work of artists otherwise as different from one another as José Gamarra of Uruguay (b. 1934) and Jacobo Borges of Venezuela (b. 1931). It is also conspicuous in the art of leading younger Mexican painters such as Alejandro Colunga (b. 1948) and Roberto Marquez (b. 1959). Significantly, these younger Mexicans owe more to the example of Rufino Tamayo (b. 1899) and to the continuing strength of Mexican folk art and custom than they do to the Muralists.

It used to be a cherished shibboleth of Western culture that the only art of the slightest interest produced in the Soviet Union was the work of artists who were completely alienated from Soviet society. Critics in the West were, nevertheless, disappointed by the exhibitions of 'unofficial' Soviet art which found their way to the other side of the Iron Curtain. The most substantial of these exhibitions is commemorated by the book *Unofficial Art from the Soviet Union* by Igor Golomshtok and Alexander Glezer, published in 1977. The text often makes curious reading in the new era of *glasnost*. However, one aspect of it remains relevant, and this is the fact that it illustrates a great medley of different styles and approaches to art, seemingly without any organic connection with one another. Now that the climate has changed so dramatically, and there is an immense and ever-increasing interest in Soviet artists of all kinds, from the most conservative (whose products are sometimes regarded as inexpensive substitutes for the Impressionists) to the most experimental, the hierarchy of development remains unsettled. It is at the moment impossible for a Western critic to tell for certain which Russian artists are to be regarded as important stylistic innovators, and which are mere camp-followers.

On the other hand, the hierarchy of American and Western European artists grows increasingly rigid, and more and more tends to be computed in terms of financial value. One of the most striking, if not one of the most reassuring artistic events of the 1980s occurred when a work by a living artist, *False Start* by Jasper Johns (b. 1930), fetched a price in excess of $17 million, ranking him as the author of one of the ten most expensive paintings ever sold at auction. In the circumstances, contemporary art can hardly complain of lack of status.

GERMAN NEO-EXPRESSIONISM

The new figuration has been more consistently associated with German artists than with those of any other national school. This association is natural enough, since the original Expressionism of the period just before and after World War I (which the new style often closely resembled) had been specifically German. Though the German Expressionists of the early modernist period undoubtedly owed something to the French Fauves, Matisse in particular, they were also conscious of deep roots in the German past. Their powerful woodcuts, for example, demonstrate their debt to the impassioned German art of the Late Gothic.

There is a kind of paradox about the revival of Expressionism in Germany which has been very little understood by non-German critics. Commentators point to the long period following World War II during which Germany, despite her rapid economic recovery and the accompanying revival of cultural activity, remained in thrall to foreign styles. They suggest that the return to national roots was very belated and that when it took place there was a sudden and complete stylistic revolution.

If this is true at all, it is only true of what happened in the Federal Republic. The revival of Expressionist painting in East Germany began very soon after the war. There were particular reasons for this revival. Expressionism had been condemned by the Nazis — the Expressionist style was what they meant to point to when they denounced the 'decadence' of modernism. The Exhibition of Degenerate Art staged in Munich in 1937 contained examples of other modernist styles, but was essentially the largest exhibition of Expressionist painting and sculpture ever to have been held in Germany up to that time.

Quite apart from their purely visceral distaste for Expressionist art, the Nazis had perfectly good political reasons for detesting it. The horrors of World War I had had the effect of politicizing the German avant-garde, and the so-called 'Second Expressionism' of the period after the war placed much greater emphasis on radical political content than the experimental art of the pre-war epoch. Paradoxically, the memory of this aspect of Expressionism may have militated against an immediate revival of the style in West Germany after World War II. German artists were tired of politics, and the Weimar Expressionists seemed too strident, and also too poignant a reminder of the dark years Germany had endured. This was not the case in the East, where the Communist regime, anxious to stress its own continuity with the heroic days of German Marxism in the 1920s and on the look-out for an effectively propagandist art, found it natural to pick up the threads of an artistic development which had been severed by Hitler's rise to power.

Werner Tübke. *Three Women*. 1983. Oil on canvas, 150 × 150 cm (59 × 59 in). Courtesy Schlesinger Gallery, New York

The two artists most favoured by the East German regime from the mid-fifties onward were Werner Tübke (b. 1929) and Willi Sitte (b. 1921). Tübke's work, heavily indebted to Dürer, Altdorfer and Hans Baldung Grien, anticipated attitudes which were to be of great importance to many non-Communist artists in the 1980s, though in this case the similarities were probably coincidental. Things were different with Willi Sitte, a powerful painter whose work is an eclectic amalgam of the Picasso of the 1940s and 1950s, Renato Guttuso and the German artists of the Second Expressionism. Sitte's art is strident and occasionally vulgar, but it is undoubtedly a powerful instrument of communication. The political propaganda

is often leavened with an effectively blatant eroticism. The way in which Sitte sometimes foreshadows the West German Neo-Expressionism of the 1970s and 1980s is very striking.

The Expressionist revival in West Germany had its start as early as the 1960s, though it was not noticed much outside Berlin. It seems to have owed a great deal to a knowledge of what was going on in the East. A pioneer of the movement was Georg Baselitz (b. 1938), who was born in East Germany and lived there until 1956. Baselitz moved to West Berlin to continue his studies because he had been expelled from the East Berlin School of Fine Arts for 'socio-political immaturity'. But his early experiences in the so-called 'free world' were scarcely happier than those he had had in the East. His first one-man show, held at the Galerie Michael Werner in Berlin in 1963, caused a tremendous scandal. The paintings he showed were figurative and not very far in style from those being produced at the same moment by Willi Sitte. The cause of offence was not the style but the content – specifically, certain erotic allusions.

These two experiences – his clash with the East Berlin authorities, and then with the public prosecutor in the other half of the city, seem to have given Baselitz a permanent feeling of revulsion for all forms of political involvement. As he said in an interview given in 1983:

Gradually the idea dawned on me that I could launch myself into painting. I thought that to do a picture I did not necessarily have to have an interesting subject. The object had no intrinsic importance any more. So I chose insignificant things... The object expresses nothing. Painting is not a means to an end. On the contrary, painting is autonomous.

In the late 1960s Baselitz's practical reaction to this train of thought was to begin painting pictures in which the image was fractured or fissured; and then to paint every image upside down. Baselitz differs from German Neo-Expressionists younger than himself in his insistence on the formal qualities of the work – on its identity as paint.

As the Neo-Expressionist style developed in Germany, and specifically in Berlin, this attitude of political detachment could not be maintained. Sometimes political symbols were used in a relatively unspecific way, as for example in some of the *Dithyramb* paintings produced by Markus Lüpertz in the 1970s and 80s, which make play with typically German motifs such as the helmet, the ear of corn and the military cap. Sometimes the political message is clear and detailed, as in the *Café Deutschland* series by Jorg Immendorf (b. 1945), which comment upon the division of Germany. These artists were, in any case, responding to an increasing political polarization within West Germany itself.

A much richer and subtler political content appeared in the work of Anselm Kiefer (b. 1945). Kiefer, though still under fifty, is generally considered to be the most important living German artist, certainly since the death of his own mentor, Joseph Beuys (1921–86). A full generation younger than Baselitz and from West, not East Germany,

Georg Baselitz. *Still no Snow*. 1988. Oil on canvas, 162 × 130 cm (63³/₄ × 51¹/₈ in). Courtesy Anthony d'Offay Gallery, London

Jorg Immendorf. *Cafe Deutchland Horerwunsch.* **1983. Oil on canvas, 150.3 × 200.8 cm (59$^1/_4$ × 79$^1/_8$ in). Private Collection**

Anselm Kiefer. *The High Priestess* (detail). 1985–9. Photographs mounted on treated lead, 75.5 × 52 × 11 cm (29³/₄ × 20¹/₂ × 4¹/₂ in). Courtesy Anthony d'Offay Gallery, London

he is more representative of what has happened to the Neo-Expressionist impulse in the German art of the 1980s. Unlike Baselitz, Kiefer never experienced the war, even as a child. Despite this lack of direct contact with traumatic events, his constant preoccupations are with the German past, with the fate of German culture, and with the heritage of Nazism.

Kiefer studied with Beuys from 1970 to 1972, and is his direct heir. However, instead of seeking completely new forms, as Beuys did throughout his career – rituals and happenings, and even direct political action – Kiefer has tried to revive traditional formats. In particular, he has given new life to a form of expression long considered obsolete: the large painting which is not a decoration but a considered public statement. The best comparisons for some of Kiefer's recent major works are Géricault's *The Raft of the Brig 'Medusa'* and Delacroix's *Massacre at Chios*, which are comments on contemporary politics of exactly the same kind.

Kiefer is notoriously reluctant to supply biographical facts about himself, and forbids direct quotation from any interviews that he gives. However, a brief and quirky 'Autobiography' written in 1976 (a chronological list of names and events covering about a page) makes it plain that his intellectual progress has been increasingly a matter of searching for his own identity as a German. In the 1960s, when Kiefer was still a student, he was able to travel widely, and his first heroes were either non-Germans such as van Gogh and Rodin, or else German cosmopolitans like the poet Rainer Maria Rilke. Kiefer has always been attracted towards what are, in German terms, dangerous areas. In the 1970s some of his work uses images taken from the operas of Wagner and the Norse Edda on which *The Ring* cycle is based. He also painted a series of pictures mythologizing enterprises of the German high command during the war – for example, Operation Sea Lion, a scheme for the invasion of England. The works in this particular series are a mixture of tones – simultaneously ironic and heroic. For instance, Kiefer recalls the fact that naval operations were sometimes planned using toy ships in a bathtub.

During this period Kiefer established himself as a landscape painter of sombre power. The devastated terrain which he so often depicted was a sacrilegious yet, at the same time, reverential gesture directed towards the mystical love of nature which is deep-rooted in German Romantic poetry and painting. Despite the disparity of scale, resemblances exist between Kiefer's work and that of Caspar David Friedrich, the leading German landscape painter of the Romantic epoch, whose work always carries strong symbolic overtones.

In the 1980s one major theme to which Kiefer returned repeatedly was the memory of the Holocaust. Many paintings use imagery taken from the poem *Todesfuge (Death Fuge)* written in a concentration camp in 1945 by the Romanian Jewish poet Paul Celan. Celan, the only member of his family to survive the camps, committed suicide in 1970. Two of the chief images in the poem are golden-haired Margarete, the personification of Aryan beauty, and Shulamith the Jewess, 'ashen-haired' because she has been cremated in a concentration-camp oven. Later in the 1980s Kiefer found another source of imagery in the overbearing neo-classical architecture designed for Hitler by Albert Speer and others, sometimes combining this theme with that of Margarete and Shulamith.

One of the ways in which Kiefer demonstrates his continuing kinship with Beuys is through his use of unortho-

Rainer Fetting. *Shower II*. 1980. Powder paint on cotton, 220 × 160 cm (86¹/₂ × 63 in). Courtesy Anthony d'Offay Gallery, London

dox materials. Beuys employed fat and felt, substances which had both symbolic and autobiographical meaning for him — their connotations included warmth, energy and protection. Kiefer's chosen materials include straw and lead. The latter has alchemical significance, and alchemy is one of Kiefer's long-standing interests. For him, the making of a work of art is a transformation of physical realities through occult means, of the kind attempted by medieval alchemists.

Rainer Fetting (b. 1949) is close to Kiefer in age, but is a far more traditional kind of artist, who perhaps demonstrates that the level of intensity present in Kiefer's work cannot be reliably sustained. Where Fetting excels is in the virtuoso handling of paint. His subject-matter covers most of the traditional genres — portraiture, nudes, landscape and cityscape. Some paintings make use of collaged elements, but this is not standard practice with Fetting as it is with Kiefer. Compared to those of the original Expressionists, Fetting's paintings, influenced by American post-war trends, are very large. The likeness between his work and that of 'classical' Expressionists — for instance Kirchner — is therefore much more striking in reproduction than it is in reality. What reads as intensity and inner agitation when seen on a small scale becomes suave and operatic on a larger one. In some of Fetting's recent cityscapes there is a telling likeness to paintings by Kokoschka using similar subject-matter. This points to a significant general resemblance. Kokoschka, an Austrian with close ties to the Dresden-based Expressionism of *Die Brücke* (a city where he in fact settled and worked for a while), began working as a very specifically Germanic artist but finished as a cosmopolitan. Fetting has followed the same path and now spends much of his time in New York. His work never possessed much political content and now almost entirely lacks it, apart from his continued protest about the existence of the Berlin Wall. The predominant impression one takes away from his recent paintings is that of an artist very much at ease with the society he inhabits.

The development and reception of German Neo-Expressionism from Baselitz to Fetting seems to form a complete trajectory — from total rejection to the fullest international acceptance. The huge success enjoyed by their elders has made things difficult for German artists of

Rainer Fetting. *Embrace at the Pier.* **1987. Oil on linen,
228 × 182 cm (89³/₄ × 71¹/₂ in). Courtesy Raab Galleries,
Berlin/London**

Thomas Schindler. *Aperlude*. 1982/4. Oil on canvas, 200 × 160 cm (78³/4 × 63 in). Courtesy Raab Galleries, Berlin/London

Thomas Schindler. *Drinker I*. 1987. Oil on canvas,
210 × 180 cm (82¹/₂ × 70³/₄ in). Courtesy Raab Gallery, London

Peter Chevalier. *The Day*. 1987. Oil on canvas,
161 × 200 cm (63¹/₂ × 78³/₄ in). Courtesy Raab Gallery, London

the newest generation, for whom Neo-Expressionism has inevitably become a kind of academic art. The most successful work produced by German artists born in the 1950s looks rather subdued in comparison to that done by their immediate predecessors. Peter Chevalier (b. 1955) and Thomas Schindler (b. 1959) are good examples of this newer and less fluent style. Both seem to have been influenced by the mysterious allegories of Max Beckmann. But there are also traces of the impact made by the later work of Giorgio de Chirico, and perhaps also that of

the Italian artists of the Trans-avantgarde. If one compares their work to that of Fetting, the general idiom is harsher and more linear, but with numerous allusions to classical forms. There was a similar development in Weimar Germany when Expressionism was challenged by the artists of the *Neue Sachlichkeit* (New Objectivity). However, both Schindler and Chevalier prefer fantastic, poetic subject-matter and show no trace of the political and social concerns which typified the art of the Weimar period and resurfaced in some Neo-Expressionist art.

ITALIAN TRANS-AVANTGARDE

Trans-avantgarde (in Italian *Trans-avant-guardia*) is a term invented by the Italian critic Achille Bonito Oliva and first used by him in an article published in the periodical *Flash Art* in the autumn of 1979. In 1980 Bonito Oliva published a book on the same theme. With these credentials, painting of the type he espoused may seem very much a phenomenon of the 1980s. The general inclination, encouraged by the inclusion of some of these Italian artists in *A New Spirit in Painting* and subsequent anthology shows following the same pattern, is to classify the movement as the Italian equivalent of German Neo-Expressionism.

This is not strictly the case. The work of the Trans-avantgarde painters can be related to problems which have preoccupied Italian artists almost throughout the century. In Italian terms it can be linked to the career of Giorgio de Chirico (1888–1978), and in particular to his later work. De Chirico is a difficult and ambiguous figure, a thorn in the flesh to many historians of modern art. He was active for a long lifetime, but the work he produced from the 1920s onwards has until recently been condemned by most critics. Even after de Chirico's death, it was given only token representation in the large retrospective exhibition organized by the Museum of Modern Art in New York in 1982 and afterwards shown at the Tate Gallery. A large number of late pictures did, however, appear in a revised version of the show which was seen in Paris and Munich. This accelerated the rehabilitation of the later de Chirico which Italian enthusiasts had begun in the 1970s.

To some extent, the neglect of de Chirico's later production was the artist's own fault. His rejection of his metaphysical period (the one the historians preferred), combined with his willingness to copy and sometimes even to fake the work of this epoch, persuaded people that anything he produced subsequently completely lacked integrity. Nor could they take seriously his strident claims that he had now returned successfully to the tradition of the Italian Old Masters. During the 1920s and 1930s de Chirico made playful use of 'antique' motifs, especially in the paintings of the *Gladiator* series, which showed classical figures battling in closed interiors, and in the *Mysterious Baths* which followed. Many of de Chirico's paintings of this time show the influence of

Sandro Chia. *Hidden Sex*. 1982. Oil and collage on panel, 126 × 113 cm (49¹/₂ × 44¹/₂ in). Courtesy Anthony d'Offay Gallery, London

Pompeian murals, not only in the themes chosen, but in a certain rapidity and sketchiness, and in a deliberate spatial discontinuity. Some examples have a very seductive air of chic; others, the Old Master pastiches especially, teeter on the edge of vulgarity, and quite often seem to fall over it.

The stylistic ambiguity of de Chirico's late work and his ironic attitude not only to the idea of the past but to the idea of 'quality' in painting seem to have exercised a great attraction over the members of the emergent Trans-avantgarde group. During the mid-1980s many other painters, especially in the United States, were to fall under the same spell.

The Trans-avantgarde artists, like each generation of Italian modernists before them, are extremely conscious of the crushing weight of the Italian past. Their painting tends to refer not to a single stylistic moment (as is the case with German Neo-Expressionism) but to all historic styles in general, as things to be interrogated, parodied

Sandro Chia. *I am a Fisherman*. 1984. Oil on canvas,
190 × 150 cm (74⁷/₈ × 50¹/₈ in). Private Collection

Francesco Clemente. *Paradigm*. 1988. Pigment on linen,
208 × 142 cm (82 × 56 in). Courtesy Sperone Westwater Gallery,
New York

Enzo Cucchi. *The House of the Barbarians*. 1982. Oil on canvas,
312.4 × 212.1 cm (123¹/₂ × 83¹/₂ in). Private Collection

Mimmo Paladino. *Untitled*. 1988. Mixed media on wood,
230 × 152.5 × 30 cm (90¹/₂ × 60 × 11⁷/₈ in). Private Collection

and disrupted. The clearest example is the work of Sandro Chia (b. 1946). In an interview with Wolfgang Fischer recorded in September 1987, Chia remarked:

The special capacity that an artist should have is to perceive what is given as a cultural tradition, to perceive this cultural reality in a more unconventional, outrageous way. It is his task, and also his social duty, not to settle for the first definition of tradition and culture, but to create the conditions for meta-morphosis, a reconsideration of something that is already present in some way, that already represents a possibility for creation. It is his task to start a new creation from an existing creation.

Chia puts this doctrine into practice by making art which is an ironic commentary on the heroics of the past. His paintings are frequently knockabout versions of class-ical myths, with rolypoly nude figures which threaten to turn into Michelin Men. The compositions are often altered quotations from established masterpieces. Chia sometimes adds an autobiographical element, and makes the artist the hero of whatever story is being told. The only Expressionist feature is the deliberate roughness of the technique. Chia's bombast, mingled though it is with flashes of ironic self-awareness, has created growing crit-ical mistrust, and his reputation, created so rapidly in the early years of the decade, looks increasingly insecure.

Francesco Clemente (b. 1952) casts his net much wider than Chia. He has been interested in non-European cul-tures since the beginning of his career. In 1975 he began to spend long periods of each year in India, and he now maintains a studio in Madras. Clemente experiments rest-lessly with whatever techniques seem indigenous to the place he is in, making woodcuts in Japan, trying to revive the now almost-extinct methods of true fresco painting when in Italy. His imagery, however, is very much of the moment – a wild mixture of allusions to different cultures and creeds. It is as if the contents of a dictionary of world mythologies have been poured into a single pot and stirred vigorously. Like Chia, Clemente frequently makes himself the hero of his own story: self-portraits abound in his production.

His work is more difficult to characterize than Chia's simply because of its diversity of style and content, but Clemente's own claims for it are considerable – he sees himself as a kind of seer, on the model of some of the key figures of early Romanticism. He praises Blake and Fuseli, for example, for being 'the first western painters to take a close look at bad taste, to see truth as bad taste'. This begs the question of whether the concept of bad taste has any reality outside the Western, and specifically the Greco-Roman tradition. Clemente also expresses sym-pathy with what he sees as the 'deliberate dilettantism' of Giorgio de Chirico, and also of Francis Picabia (an artist whose career followed very much the same pattern as de Chirico's in the 1920s and 1930s, and who has been regarded as another ancestor of 1980s 'bad painting'). All this adds up to a subtle and provocative personality, but Clemente is also an artist who produces far too much which is derivative and superficial. Many of the Indian works, for example, are little more than large-scale pastiches of traditional Indian bazaar-painting, significant only because they are part of the opening out to non-European cultures which has been one of the characteristics of the 1980s.

The third of the so-called 'Three Cs', Enzo Cucchi (b. 1949), is the artist of the group who comes closest to some aspects of German Neo-Expressionism, and especially to the work of Anselm Kiefer. Like Kiefer, 'his pictures depict, or incorporate actual references to, the elements of earth, water and fire, such as soil and charred wood.' These, we are told (the description comes from the biography of Cucchi in the catalogue of the great survey show of Italian twentieth-century art mounted at the Royal Academy in London in 1989), 'evoke the primeval and rejuvenating forces of nature, the cycles of death and destruction, rebirth and rejuvenation'. Such very large claims deserve to be met with a certain scepticism, and in fact Cucchi's work can sometimes be coarsely rhetorical. At his best, however, he is a powerful artist.

The most convincing of the Trans-avantgarde painters, somewhat isolated in style from the others, is Mimmo Paladino (b.1948). Paladino comes from the south of Italy. He was born near Benevento and brought up in Naples, and he has remained attached to his roots there. His painting is historicist in a more focused and less frivolous way than that of Clemente and Chia. His primary sources are Italian: he draws on Greco-Roman, early Christian and Romanesque art, with an apparent preference for their more primitive and provincial manifestations.

Paladino takes his lead from these models by reducing his palette to oppositions of a few strong earth tones, plus black and white. Some paintings are monochrome, or all but monochrome. Christian subject-matter is often para-phrased. One favourite theme is a version of the Last Supper, but the feast is diabolized, so that it becomes a witches' conclave. The hints of the blasphemous, which are common currency in Paladino's work, go hand in hand with a kind of animism. Animals sometimes perform human actions, as they do in Romanesque church decor-ation. Paladino's paintings also celebrate a cult of death, with many representations of skeletons, death's heads and bogies of all kinds. The result does not altogether escape the dangers of artificiality – Paladino's primitivism can seem a bit cooked up, especially in the sculptures which he produces in addition to his paintings. But he gives an effective new twist to the Italian tradition of respecting and studying, yet at the same time perverting the art of the past.

If one compares the Italian painters of the Trans-avantgarde to their German Neo-Expressionist counter-parts, it becomes clear that the Italians lack complex pol-itical content, and concern themselves more with creating archetypes which can be seen as reflections of psychic states common to everyone, not just to men and women of one nationality. They are also much more interested in precise nuances of style, and have a greater tendency to stylistic pluralism.

BRITISH PAINTING

In the 1970s, it was British sculpture which seemed to attest to the continuing vitality of British art. By general consent, British painting had sunk into the doldrums after the excitement provided by the British Pop Art movement of the previous decade. Certain painters were ignored by critics because they seemed to have no place on the then current map of the various avant-garde movements and their relationships.

One artist marginalized by this pattern of thinking was Lucian Freud (b.1922). Freud, grandson of Sigmund Freud, the founder of psychoanalysis, was born in Berlin. His family emigrated to Britain in 1933 and Freud became a British citizen in 1939. His early work was in the Neo-Romantic idiom fashionable in Britain before and just after World War II. It was conspicuously brittle and mannered. During the 1950s his style began to change towards something broader and more painterly, and by the 1960s this stylistic change was complete. Important influences on him were Francis Bacon and the great seventeenth-century Dutch portraitist Frans Hals.

Most of Freud's mature pictures are portraits, or nudes with a portrait-like quality. Bacon taught Freud to look at the frequent lack of synchronicity between the bony armature and the envelope of flesh that covers it; Hals provided lessons in directness. As a result of his studying these artists, Freud's work acquired a deliberately raw quality. It was not technically Expressionist, but it had a similar psychological directness and disregard for social convention.

Throughout the 1960s and for most of the 1970s Freud's work seemed irrelevant to what was happening on either the purely British or the international scene. It did not change in any important respect in the 1980s, though at the beginning of the decade he did produce the largest and most ambitious canvas he had ever attempted – the *Large Interior W11 (After Watteau)*. The group of figures, drawn from his friends, is a paraphrase of Watteau's *Pierrot Content* in the Thyssen-Bornemisza collection in Lugano. They are, however, placed in the kind of sleazy studio interior familiar from a number of Freud's canvases, and not in the park-like open-air setting which Watteau provided in the original. The effect is strained, and Freud sensibly reverted to working on his more modest customary scale.

Frank Auerbach. *Head of J Y M.* 1987. Oil on canvas, 36.8 × 41.3 cm (14¹/₄ × 16¹/₄ in). Private Collection

What did alter during the decade was the public reception of Freud's work. Its latent Expressionist qualities were recognized following the rise of Neo-Expressionism in Germany. At the same time, it could suddenly be seen that Freud's explorations were not entirely solitary even in England, but had things in common with the work of other British artists, particularly that of two pupils of David Bomberg – Frank Auerbach and Leon Kossoff.

Frank Auerbach (b.1931) is also a German Jewish refugee. He was sent to England as a child in 1939, and he lost his whole family in the Holocaust. Soon after World War II he came into contact with Bomberg and attended the classes which the latter taught at the Borough Polytechnic in London. Here he absorbed Bomberg's very personal variety of 'slow Expressionism', a way of painting best described as Expressionist brushwork allied to the painstaking exploration of external reality associated with Cézanne. From the beginning Auerbach was interested in searching for a true equivalence between the thing seen

Leon Kossoff. *Outside the Booking Hall, Kilburn Underground.* 1980. Oil on board, 183 × 152.4 cm (72 × 60 in). Courtesy Fischer Fine Art Ltd, London

and the marks which appear on the painted surface. He wanted not merely to capture reality in paint but actually to re-create it on the canvas. He tackled the same narrow range of motifs with obsessive persistence – his usual subjects were heads and single figures (the same models sat for him patiently, year after year), and a few landscapes and cityscapes. In each work the paint was piled up in thick ropes and layers. The motif was depicted again and again on the same surface, partially scraped down between sessions, and then yet again repainted. Like Freud, Auerbach narrowed the range of his art so as to exclude all transcendental overtones. It was the painter's relationship to quotidian facts which counted.

Leon Kossoff (b. 1926) is Jewish too, but his family were Russian immigrants and had been settled in Britain for some time before the artist was born. He, too, became a pupil of Bomberg at the Borough Polytechnic, and his technique and attitudes are very close to Auerbach's, with perhaps a wider range of subject-matter and a greater latitude for the introduction of personal sentiment. Kossoff has painted many pictures of his father, for example (these correspond to a series of portraits of his mother painted by Freud).

At a first glance, Auerbach and Kossoff appear to be Expressionist painters; Freud, too, has at least a tenuous link to Expressionism. The fact that two of the three are of German origin may have helped to reinforce the idea that theirs is an art which offers parallels to the new movement in Germany. The stylistic similarities are largely coinci-

dental. There is, however, one basic objective which the new Germans have in common with these much longer-established British artists: the search for a national identity.

Today, Freud, Auerbach and Kossoff produce work which is intimately connected with the painting produced in Britain in the opening years of the twentieth century. Through Bomberg, the latter two have a historical link with Vorticism. Their instinctive allegiance, however, is to the artists of the Camden Town Group, who clustered around Walter Richard Sickert (1860–1942), another foreign-born painter who made himself a consciously British persona.

One of the most significant exhibitions of the early 1980s, so far as younger British arts were concerned, was the *Late Sickert* show mounted by the Arts Council of Great Britain at the Hayward Gallery in 1981. The catalogue contains a foreword written by Auerbach in which he says:

If one were to ascribe a development to him, one might say that Sickert became less interested in composition, that is, in selection, arrangement and presentation, devoted himself more and more to a direct transformation of whatever came accidentally to hand and engaged his interest, and accepted the haphazard variety of his unprocessed subject-matter.

As it happens, this almost exactly characterizes the nature of Auerbach's own art, and applies fairly exactly, in addition, to Freud and Kossoff.

The formation of a new central group of senior artists tended to isolate others who might themselves have hoped to be part of the centre. However, one must except Francis Bacon (b. 1909) from this group, who has never aspired to centrality of any sort, and who, though attracting numerous imitators both in Britain and abroad (his work was particularly influential in Latin America after it was shown at the São Paulo Bienale), has never wanted to form a school. Bacon's painting, like Freud's, continued during the 1980s to follow a path which the artist had laid down for it a long time previously. The only scarcely discernible change was increased boldness of handling.

Howard Hodgkin (b. 1932) had been the odd-man-out amongst the artists of his generation in the days of Pop Art, and continued to be so now. Though his hermetic

Bill Jacklin. *Franks.* 1988. Pastel on paper,
105.4 × 75.5 cm (41¹/₂ × 29³/₄ in). **Private Collection**

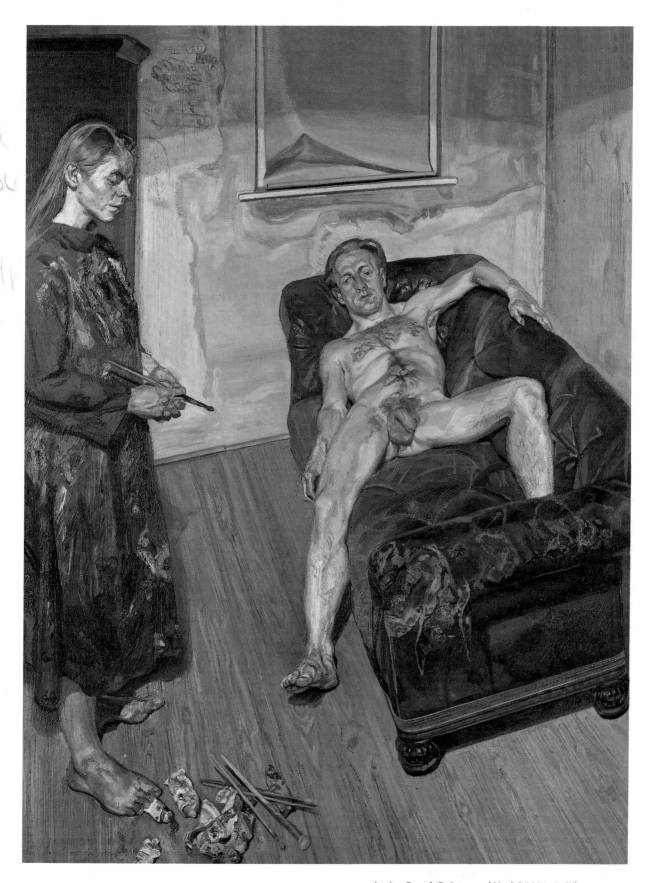

Lucian Freud. *Painter and Model.* 1986–7. Oil on canvas,
159.6 × 120.7 cm (65 × 47¹/₂ in). Private Collection

Leon Kossoff. *Here Comes the Diesel*. **1987. Oil on board,
61.6 × 55.9 cm (24¹/₂ × 22 in). Courtesy Anthony d'Offay Gallery,
London**

Frank Auerbach. *Head of Catherine Lampert*. **1986. Oil on canvas, 51.4 × 47 cm (20¹/₄ × 18¹/₂ in). Courtesy Marlborough Fine Art, London**

Howard Hodgkin. *Down in the Valley*. Oil on wood, 73.7 × 91.4 cm (29 × 36 in). Courtesy M. Knoedler & Co., New York

compositions – memories of interiors with people in them and of other scenes – had sometimes been loosely described as Expressionist in the past, they did not fit the Neo-Expressionist ethos because of their lack of rhetoric. In the 1980s Hodgkin (always a slow worker) slightly increased his production and the pictures became less hermetic, with the figurative elements more clearly discernible. Reaction to his work was altered less by any change in his approach or methods, than by a shift in public taste (exactly as in Freud's case). What affected reactions to Hodgkin's work was the rising interest in the Bloomsbury Group. Attention had long been concentrated on Bloomsbury writers such as Virginia Woolf and Lytton Strachey, but this now spilled over to include the leading Bloomsbury artists Vanessa Bell and Duncan Grant. As Bloomsbury's output in the visual arts became better known and better understood, Hodgkin came to

seem more and more like a scion of the group, and in particular a descendant of the decorative painting done in connection with the Omega Workshops. This, in turn, tended to stress his fairly distant, but nevertheless very real connection with Matisse.

Two highly successful younger painters also remained in isolation. One of these was Bill Jacklin (b. 1943). Once an abstract artist of crystalline elegance, he was now established as a creator of complex figurative scenes. An exhibition in the summer of 1988 at Marlborough Fine Art, London, of Jacklin's recent work devoted to New York cityscapes and interiors, showed that he has a connection with some of the realists who had flourished in New York during the 1930s, notably the twin brothers Moses and Raphael Soyer. The realism practised by the Soyers was always celebratory rather than critical – it did not have the harsh edge of the work done by their New York predecessors of the Ash Can School, or of that of Sickert and the Camden Town Group. Jacklin is content to celebrate what he sees in the same fashion.

Bruce McLean. *Untitled.* **1986. Acrylic, enamel and collage on canvas, 281.9 × 200.7 cm (111 × 79 in). Courtesy Anthony d'Offay Gallery, London**

Bill Jacklin. *The Desk 35th Precinct.* **1988. Oil on canvas, 198.1 × 198.1 cm (78 × 78 in). Courtesy Marlborough Fine Art, London**

Bruce McLean (b. 1944) came to the fore in the 1970s as a performance artist – one equipped with a sympathetic sense of irony. His painting developed out of the settings he created for his own performances. Though he is Glaswegian by birth, he has lived in London since 1963, and is not connected with the sudden blossoming of Scottish painting which occurred in the 1980s. When his paintings first appeared, they were immediately hailed as a development of Neo-Expressionism, on a par with what was being done in Germany, and they were vigorously marketed in New York on that basis. In fact, they seem to have little to do with any kind of Expressionism – they are full of bold gestures, decorative and theatrical, but they are not intense or filled with *Angst*. It is typical of the nature of McLean's talent that he has also successfully turned his hand to decorating pottery. His ceramics recall some of Picasso's best efforts in this field – they have the same wit, and the same terse economy.

Gilbert and George (b. 1943 & 1942) are also graduates of the performance art scene. They used to describe everything they produced as sculpture, and every action of their daily lives was meant to be regarded as sculpture too. In the 1980s their main effort went into the production of large photo-pieces. These are not paintings and should not be described as such, but they function in much the same way. Because of their explosive content, these photo-pieces have often aroused controversy. Some use religious imagery in a way which may seem blasphemous to believers; others contain erotic images, such as phalluses, or seem to celebrate neo-fascism. The stiffly polite and dignified demeanour of the artists has been an added irritant to their critics. The stringent discipline and unity of their style has obscured the fact that their work pulls in several different directions. Some of it seems to be the product of simple Warholian voyeurism; some is narcissistic self-celebration; some is filled with genuine social and moral indignation; some is deliberately provocative in the traditional fashion of avant-garde art. While it is a little difficult to decide on the aesthetic merits of what they do, there can be no doubt that it is an honest reflection of its time. The dislike it arouses should often be redirected to the surrounding political and economic circumstances – Gilbert and George merely show the spectator, with devastating clarity, what he knew existed

Bruce McLean. *Untitled.* **1986. Acrylic, collage and metallic paint on canvas, 260 × 198.5 cm (102¹/2 × 78¹/4 in). Courtesy Anthony d'Offay Gallery, London**

Howard Hodgkin. *On the Riviera*. 1987–8. Oil on board,
104.5 × 111.5 cm (41^1/$_8$ × 43^7/$_8$ in). Courtesy M. Knoedler & Co.,
New York

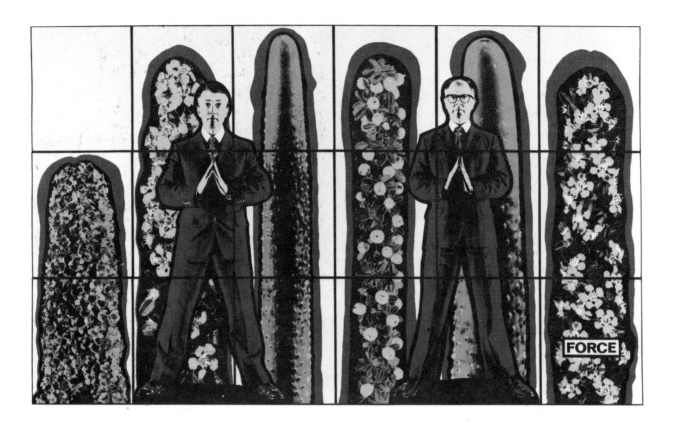

**Gilbert and George. *Force*. 1988. 27 × 381 cm (89¹/₄ × 150 in).
Courtesy Anthony d'Offay Gallery, London**

but had up to that moment managed to ignore. They have also shown particular sensitivity to contemporary issues – a faculty demonstrated by their Crusaid exhibition of 1989, when all the proceeds went to Aids charities. Gilbert and George are even more isolated stylistically than the other artists discussed in the second half of this chapter, but in the future they will almost certainly be seen as an important episode within the cultural history of the decade.

NEW SCOTTISH PAINTING

The loudest assertion of national identity to be made by younger British painters in the 1980s came not from England, but from Scotland. Throughout the twentieth century Scottish art has struggled to assert the fact that it has a different tradition from the English one, and therefore a separate personality. Between 1910 and 1930, for example, there was a powerful Post-Impressionist tendency in Scottish art. Among its chief representatives were S.J. Peploe (1871–1935), F.C.B. Cadell (1883–1937) and J.D. Fergusson (1874–1931). Peploe and Fergusson spent much time in France, and their work tends to be a direct response to French exemplars such as Cézanne and the Fauves (especially Matisse), without much reference to what was going on in England at the same moment. Until recently, the Scottish Colourists, as they are known, tended in turn to be ignored by the historians of British modernism. The show *British Art in the 20th Century*, mounted by the Royal Academy in 1987, not only omitted the Colourists but paid little attention to Scottish art in general. Those artists of Scottish birth who were included (a tiny handful) had long separated themselves from Scotland.

The current revival of interest in Scottish painting owes much to two artists who form a fascinating and instructive contrast. One is John Bellany (b.1942). Bellany was born in the Scottish fishing village of Port Seton and attended the Edinburgh College of Art. In 1965 he moved to London, where he continued his training at the Royal College of Art, and since then he has based himself in the south, teaching until recently at various London art schools.

Throughout his career, however, Bellany has retained an ineradicable Scottishness. Much of his imagery relates to his childhood and youth. In dealing with it, he was able to turn to a native tradition of 'Scottish Expressionism', or at least of boldly brushed colouristic painting of a kind associated with artists such as William Gillies (1898–1973), William MacTaggart (b.1903) and Joan Eardley (1921–63). The Expressionist impulse in Bellany's painting was focused and made more specific by his admiration for the work of German artist Max Beckmann (1884–1950), who is one of the important hidden influences in the art of the 1980s, not only in Germany, but internationally. In particular, Bellany was greatly

John Bellany. *Self-Portrait with Juliet.* 1981. Oil on canvas, 172.7 × 152.4 cm (68 × 60 in). Private Collection

influenced by Beckmann's triptychs, with their mysterious and fantastic imagery, to such an extent he quite often adopted the triptych format himself.

Bellany's work was featured in quite a number of mixed exhibitions held in Britain during the 1970s. It is symptomatic that he was selected for an Arts Council Touring Exhibition entitled *Scottish Realism* in 1971, and for another called *Scottish Expressionism* in 1977. The difference in titles does indicate a stylistic shift in Bellany's work, but is far more indicative of the change of artistic climate which was taking place in Britain during the decade. Bellany was, however, surprisingly slow to make an international breakthrough. His first solo exhibition in New York did not take place until 1982, and the venue was a little-known private gallery. He is, in consequence, less celebrated than the German Neo-Expressionists who are his exact contemporaries, and whose work in many respects resembles his. He is also less fêted than Scottish painters substantially younger than himself.

John Bellany. *The Quack*. 1988. Oil on canvas,
182.8 × 243.8 cm (72 × 96 in). Courtesy Fischer Fine Art Ltd,
London

Steven Campbell. *Three Men of Exactly the Same Size in an Unequal Room*. 1987.
Oil on canvas, 249 × 277 cm (98 × 109 in). Collection: Leeds City Art Gallery.
Courtesy Marlborough Fine Art, London

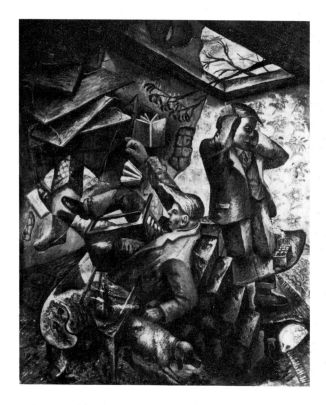

Steven Campbell. *'Twas once an Architect's Office in Wee Nook.* 1984. Oil on canvas, 292 × 241 cm (115 × 95 in). Collection Bette Ziegler, New York

Peter Howson. *Self-Portrait.* 1987. Oil on canvas, 105 × 89 cm (41·1/2 × 35 in). Courtesy Flowers East, London

Peter Howson. *The Psycho Squad.* 1989. Oil on canvas, 214 × 274.5 cm (84 1/4 × 108 in). Courtesy Flowers East, London

The other artist who played a key role in the emergence of a new Scottish scene is Steven Campbell (b. 1953). Campbell's background is significantly different from Bellany's. He spent seven years as a fitter in a steelworks, then attended Glasgow College of Art, which is still housed in the magnificent and aggressive Art Nouveau building designed for it by Charles Rennie Mackintosh (1868–1928). Instead of making his way to London when he graduated, Campbell migrated across the Atlantic, and he lived and worked for five years in the United States. His first solo exhibition was with the well-respected Barbara Toll Gallery in New York's SoHo, and he had another show the same year at the John Weber Gallery. By the end of 1986 he had had exhibitions in Chicago, Munich, Minneapolis, Washington DC, Berlin, Geneva and San Francisco, as well as in London and Edinburgh – a good example of the rapid international exposure now available to successful young artists.

Campbell's work is much less Expressionist than that of Bellany. Both the drawing and the actual handling of paint have a lot in common with that of German artists like Peter Chevalier and Thomas Schindler, who are his exact contemporaries. However, Campbell's compositions tend to be both more capricious and more complex. Campbell begins with a single image, then develops the picture through a process of free association. The poses and gestures of his figures are deliberately conventionalized: whatever is shown is presented with humorous

irony. Nevertheless Campbell, having so firmly ignored England and English institutions when planning his career strategy, remains obsessed with English (not Scottish) culture. Gainsborough and the writer P.G. Wodehouse both play an important part in his quirky personal mythology. His stocky figures are dressed in the

**Ken Currie. *In the City Bar*. 1987. Oil on canvas,
210.8 × 370.8 cm (83 × 146 in). Collection Susan Kasen and
Robert D. Summer, New York**

tweedy outfits of England in the 1930s, and inhabit the
facetious yet slightly sinister universe of W.H. Auden's
early poetic charade, *Paid On Both Sides*. The comparison
with Auden is suggestive – Campbell remains helplessly
attached to a world which in theory he dislikes and
condemns, which was precisely Auden's situation.

The work of the two artists with whom Campbell is
most closely associated, Peter Howson (b. 1958) and Ken
Currie (b. 1960), seems straightforward in comparison.
Howson, though recognized as a leading member of the
new Scottish school, was in fact born in London and
moved to Scotland when he was a child. His training at
the Glasgow School of Art was broken by a period when
he dropped out and did various odd jobs, including a stint
in the British army. This seems to have had a lasting effect
on Howson's imagination, since he tends to depict an
exaggeratedly masculine world, often one with sado-
masochistic overtones. His most impressive pictures
show not thuggish soldiers or boxers (though these also
feature largely) but Glasgow down-and-outs, who are
presented as heroic yet powerless, tragic rejects of capital-
ist society who have found reserves of stoic courage with
which to resist their fate.

Currie began as a student of social sciences before going
to art school. When he began to paint, he was at first a
disciple of the Scottish Colourist tradition, but soon

rejected this in favour of work with a strong narrative content. Currie's artistic exemplars are impeccably left-wing
– among them are Otto Dix and Max Beckmann (though
he rejects the fantastic side of the latter), Fernand Léger in
his pro-Communist and post-Cubist phase, and the Mexican Muralist Diego Rivera. More and more he has tended
to make his work a mythologization of Glasgow itself.
One sequence of large drawings Currie describes as 'a
flickering black and white newsreel of class struggle on
the Clyde in the twentieth century, seen through the eyes
of a man who has been at the sharp end of the struggle all
of his life.'

Currie's large compositions, technically very accomplished, are amongst the most convincing things of their
type to have been produced in the 1980s. He shows real
control over big spaces and the ability to orchestrate many
figures and their accoutrements into an intricate and coherent whole. What is perhaps more questionable is the
relationship between his art, its contemporary setting,
and the ideology he professes. Currie says that he has the
desire to find a new and less doctrinaire equivalent for
Soviet and Eastern European Socialist Realism, but puts
this idea forward at a time when Socialist Realism itself is
in the process of being totally rejected in its countries of
origin. He works in a city which has recently become celebrated, not for continuing dereliction, but for a dramatic
economic and cultural revival. His commitment to
Socialist Realism seems nostalgic in view of the changes
now taking place both in Britain and abroad.

Peter Howson. *A Wing and a Prayer.* **1987. Oil on canvas,
244 × 213 cm (96 × 83³/₄ in). Courtesy Flowers East, London**

Ken Currie. *Departure*. 1987. Oil on canvas, 213 × 366 cm
(84 × 144 in). Courtesy Raab Galleries, Berlin/London

NEW ENGLISH PAINTING

English painting in the 1980s has been considerably more romantic in tone than its Scottish equivalent, less stylistically coherent, and without the same orientation towards political and social issues. Two of the most successful artists have been Christopher Le Brun (b. 1951) and Ian McKeever (b. 1946). Le Brun came to prominence in 1979 as a prize-winner in the biennial John Moores Exhibition held in Liverpool, and held his first one-man exhibition in London in 1980. Since then his work has been widely shown internationally.

Christopher Le Brun. *Grove.* 1987. Oil on canvas, 106.7 × 266.6 cm (90 × 105 in). Courtesy Nigel Greenwood Gallery, London

Le Brun's original influences, when he was still a student, were the American Abstract Expressionists, for example the earlier work of Philip Guston. But by the beginning of the 1980s he had begun to paint mythological landscapes, thus returning to what some critics think of as a primary source for Abstract Expressionism – the work of J.M.W. Turner. Le Brun himself seems to have been attracted by the canvases where Turner comes closest to the Symbolist movement – for example, *The Angel Standing in the Sun*, shown at the Royal Academy in 1846. Critics have also detected resemblances between Le Brun's work and that of Arnold Böcklin and Gustave Moreau. Many of the paintings produced in the first half of the 1980s feature superb horses, often winged, so perhaps

one should also point to a possible connection with de Chirico, who during the inter-war period produced a long series of compositions showing horses on the beach. Le Brun's work is unashamedly full of references to classical and medieval literature – to the heroes of Ancient Greece and Rome, and to Sir Bedevere, Sir Tristram and the other members of King Arthur's Round Table. This subject-matter and Le Brun's nostalgic opulence of style supply two good reasons for his popularity with collectors on both sides of the Atlantic.

Much tougher, and owing more to the Conceptual Art of the 1970s, are the landscape paintings of Ian McKeever, who is somewhat older than Le Brun but has been slower to win international acclaim. His approach to landscape is through photography – blown-up photographs fragmented and collaged on to canvas, a technique also used on some occasions by Anselm Kiefer. The scenes McKeever prefers are wild and desolate, and over the years his treatment of the photographic source material, which he overpaints and now almost completely conceals, has become increasingly stormy and dramatic. Of all the painters in England now using landscape imagery, he is perhaps the most powerful.

Another Turner disciple, but one who approaches this source from a completely different angle, is Thérèse Oulton (b. 1953). Oulton produces paintings which look landscape-like in the finished result but do not seem to use landscape as a direct source. The composition grows sequentially from the marks the artist puts on the canvas – that is, one mark suggests another, without reference to objective reality. What seems to be an influence here is Turner's handling of paint, rather than his subject-matter.

Andrzej Jackowski (b. 1947) represents an image-based approach, perhaps more definitely so than any of the three painters mentioned so far. He therefore stands for a different aspect of the new English romanticism. Jackowski was born in Wales but his parents were Polish, and he spoke almost nothing but Polish until he was seven years old. He thus, like Lucian Freud in an earlier generation, retains elements of the outsider, in the sense that he has emotional access to a culture other than the native one. Jackowski's early training was at the Camberwell School of Art during the 1960s, and was strictly in the English

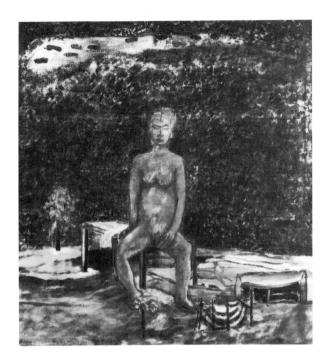

Andrzej Jackowski. *Bride/The Hatching Ground*. 1988. Oil on canvas, 152.5 × 142 cm (60 × 56 in). Collection Contemporary Art Society. Courtesy Marlborough Fine Art, London

John Keane. *The Exchange*. 1985. Oil on canvas, 211 × 168 cm (83 × 66 in). Courtesy Angela Flowers Gallery, London

realist tradition. When Jackowski moved from London to Cornwall to study at the Falmouth School of Art, he came into contact with the poet Peter Redgrove, and this had a liberating effect on his work, putting him on the path to the kind of symbolic figuration he now uses.

The painter-critic Timothy Hyman, in a conversation with Jackowski which is printed as the preface to the catalogue of the latter's 1989 exhibition at the Marlborough Gallery, London, notes that the events in Jackowski's paintings seem to take place 'in a time before or after or *outside* our civilization'. Jackowski corrects him by suggesting that his work is a kind of 'archaic fiction'. Certainly his paintings usually seem to deal with mysterious legendary events.

One recent influence which Jackowski himself notes in his own work is that of de Chirico's one-time comrade in the *Pittura Metafisica* movement in Italy, Carlo Carrà (1881–1966). The consistently dark, glowing tonality of Jackowski's paintings, and his frequent use of images of large, looming heads, also bear likeness to certain paintings by a more recent Italian artist, Enzo Cucchi. This illustrates how Jackowski's work is Expressionist as well as Symbolist. It is significant, for example, that he was included in a touring show entitled *The Subjective Eye*, which travelled to a number of British galleries in 1981–2, and which was perhaps the first attempt to identify the new Expressionist current insofar as it affected British art. Even today, Jackowski seems to be one of the British painters who comes closest to the aims and ideas of continental Neo-Expressionism.

John Keane (b. 1954) has a different relationship to Expressionism from that which appears in Jackowski's work, and a far more superficial one. What links him to aspects of Expressionism is the lively painterliness of his handling – he is a most attractive user of paint as a material, and his paintings are also notable for their freshness of colour and for the skill with which Keane manages to incorporate various collage elements, such as pieces of newspaper, without compromising the integrity of the picture surface. These skills are put to the service of a talent for ironic reportage. A recent series of paintings devoted to the theme of Nicaragua (which Keane visited in order to paint them) was very far from the kind of propaganda painting which subjects of this kind usually evoke from Neo-Expressionist artists.

The new British school of the 1980s produced a number of gifted women artists, in addition to Thérèse Oulton. This is a significant phenomenon in a country which has usually been somewhat hostile to women's creativity in the visual arts, if not in literature. Two of

Ian McKeever. *Through the Ice Lens.* **1986. Oil and photograph
on canvas, 200 × 170 cm (86³/₄ × 66³/₄ in). Courtesy Nigel
Greenwood Gallery, London**

Thérèse Oulton. *Viscous Circle*. **1989. Oil on canvas,
228.6 × 182.9 cm (90 × 72 in). Private Collection. Courtesy
Marlborough Fine Art, London**

Eileen Cooper. *Baby Talk.* **1985. Oil on canvas, 121.9 × 91.4 cm
(48 × 36 in). Courtesy Benjamin Rhodes Gallery, London**

Amanda Faulkner. *Upright Woman*. 1985/6. Acrylic on canvas,
183 × 153 cm (72 × 60¼ in). Courtesy Angela Flowers Gallery,
London

Eileen Cooper. *Last Tango*. 1988. Acrylic on paper, 120 × 80 cm (47¹/₂ × 31¹/₂ in). Courtesy Benjamin Rhodes Gallery, London

John Kirby. *Family Ties*. 1988. Oil on canvas, 204.5 × 158.8 cm (80¹/₂ × 62¹/₂ in). Courtesy Flowers East, London

these artists are Eileen Cooper (b. 1953) and Amanda Faulkner (b. 1953). Both make work which is consistently bolder in style than that of most of their male colleagues. Cooper's art is largely autobiographical, concerned with topics such as the birth of her children. She makes use of personal events as the starting point in her search for universal female archetypes. Amanda Faulkner works in a very similar vein. One of her frequent themes is the idea of the double − of two opposing or conflicting selves. She also explores other aspects of duality, such as love of yet hostility towards children.

Towards the end of the 1980s, British painting seemed to be moving away from its predominantly romantic-expressionist idiom. Two examples of this shift are John Kirby (b. 1949) and Ansel Krut (b. 1959). When compared with other British painters who are their contemporaries, both come from unusual backgrounds. Kirby was a late starter in art. A Liverpool Catholic, he worked for a period as assistant director of Boys Town, Calcutta, and later as a probation officer in south London. His paintings, which have a strong plasticity but which are fairly tight in technique, have links to those produced by *Neue Sachlichkeit* artists in Weimar Germany. Neverthe-

less, and despite the artist's background in social work, they have no trace of political content but are instead deeply and introvertedly personal. Most of them explore what Kirby speaks of as the two chief formative influences on his life: his Catholic upbringing and problems of sexual identity. Many are self-portraits (one might say, more accurately, self-representations). One typical example shows an older self keeping company with a younger one. Others show a figure who can be identified as the artist wearing women's clothes. These strange and disturbing paintings are amongst the most memorable to have been produced in Britain in recent years.

Ansel Krut was born in South Africa and studied at the University of the Witwatersrand in Johannesburg. He then lived and worked in Paris before coming to London to study at the Royal College of Art. His work, often small in scale, shows the influence of the more fantastic side of Goya, and perhaps also that of the American Jules Pascin, (1885–1930). Many of Krut's paintings are

**Ansel Krut. *The Student of Philosophies*. 1988. Oil on linen,
100 × 120 cm (39³/₈ × 47¹/₄ in). Courtesy Fischer Fine Art, London**

extremely erotic, with undertones as disturbing as those
to be found in the work of John Kirby. A series produced
in 1988 shows an adolescent girl, nude, melancholy and
passive to the point of torpor, being man handled by an
older man or men. The suggestion is often that she is
being treated as a ventriloquist's dummy. These images
are exquisitely painted. Krut uses a tightly controlled
range of subdued tones, the flesh slightly ashen, the backgrounds greenish-grey or rosy grey. Like Kirby's, his
paintings stick in the memory and find a disturbing place
there.

AMERICAN EQUIVALENTS FOR NEO-EXPRESSIONISM

It is now generally recognized that art in the United States underwent important changes in the 1980s. The exact nature of these changes is not so widely agreed. It seems to me that the only way in which we can understand the most recent American painting and sculpture is by comparing it both to the art of Europe, and to the art which provides its background in America itself. A brief historical summary is therefore required.

In the 1940s, Abstract Expressionism with the work of Pollock, de Kooning, Rothko and others established the international dominance of the New York school. Though it owed much to European Surrealism, and especially to the 'gestural' or 'calligraphic' wing of Surrealist painting (André Masson, Joan Miró and Matta), Abstract Expressionism pushed things much further than Surrealism had ever dared to do. In particular, it took the idea of automatism, and applied it to the creation of paintings rather than works of literature.

Certain aspects of Abstract Expressionism were soon recognized as having a specific relationship to American life in the 1940s and 1950s. In tune with the prosperity which now prevailed in the United States, it explicitly rejected the social concerns which had preoccupied the immediately previous generation of American artists, and reverted to the nineteenth-century concept of a 'frontier' which could be pushed forward without respite into unknown territory. This frontier, however, was psychological rather than geographical. Abstract Expressionist theory emphasized complete freedom of expression, and it was the artist's duty to record the uncensored motions of his own psyche. Each painting was seen as the product of a creative personality standing completely alone. The relevance of Abstract Expressionist attitudes to the individualism characteristic of American society was perhaps more clearly recognized by European critics than American ones.

The dominance of New York was not threatened when Abstract Expressionism was challenged by newer styles. In fact, these styles made New York more rather than less important as a point of reference. Some of the material they used came from the life of the city itself, and, like Abstract Expressionism, they depended on New York galleries, public and private, for initial exposure and subsequent validation. The most significant of these successor styles were the Neo-Dada of Robert Rauschenberg and Jasper Johns, and the American variety of Pop Art.

The new generation of American artists, in contrast to their predecessors, featured specifically American images in their work. Johns used the American flag and the map of the United States for some of his most acclaimed early paintings. The Pop artists were fascinated by the icons of American mass culture: comic-strips, images of film stars, products like Coca-Cola and Campbell's soup. Much of what they did had a close relationship to American advertising; some Pop painters, such as Warhol and Rosenquist, actually began their careers working in the advertising industry. However, though Pop referred to the social context, it was careful not to criticize it. It was celebratory or, at the least, neutral. The sole, and striking, exceptions, were Warhol's *Disaster* paintings.

During the 1970s, New York was more successful than ever as a market-place for contemporary art, and transactions became increasingly international. Within the United States, collecting the latest art was now a prestigious activity, and new artists found eager customers. As the impetus behind Pop Art faded, a number of younger artists began to concentrate on something which had always been implicit within it – an investigation of the nature of imagery, and thus, by implication, of the nature of art itself. Art-about-art took many forms, but much was Conceptual or Minimalist. As a result, the flourishing commercial impulse just described was confronted with a product whose chief qualities were often puritan reticence and stringency.

In these circumstances it is not surprising that the work of the German Neo-Expressionists and the Italian Trans-avantgarde met a warm welcome in New York. The return to conventional formats and the greater variety of content were alike greeted with relief. The one difficulty was that this flood of imports from Europe seemed to threaten the American hegemony which most of the New York art world still took for granted. It is not surprising that certain American artists were soon singled out as representatives of the new movement. One was Julian Schnabel (b. 1951). He was one of only two American Neo-Expressionists to be selected for inclusion in the Royal Academy's *A New Spirit in Painting*.

The identification with Neo-Expressionism was accepted without demur at the time, not only by commentators but by the artist himself. Today, however, Schnabel's likeness to the new European art seems a lot less obvious. For example, there is a great difference in attitude towards concepts such as nationality and rootedness, both so important in Europe. There is no doubt that Schnabel feels himself to be specifically American, just as Anselm Kiefer feels himself to be specifically German. But the two artists explore these parallel identifications in different ways. Kiefer tries to find a perspective which will enable him to define and comment upon German cultural and political history. Schnabel's historical and cultural attitudes are less complicated. They are well described by Richard Francis in his catalogue preface for the Schnabel exhibition held at the Tate Gallery in 1982:

His predilection for literature for instance is for the 'wild men': he cites Artaud, Bukowski, Cesar Vallejo and most recently the convicted murderer Jack Henry Abbott. All these men have audacity; they are positively anti-bourgeois and display their rebellion and suffering openly.

Schnabel's own anti-bourgeois credentials are doubtful in the extreme, not least because of his quest for and obvious pleasure in material success. But, while his political, social and literary attitudes are unsophisticated, his purely artistic ones are not. His work shows an intimate knowledge of the way in which American art has developed since the heroic days of Abstract Expressionism, and contains an eclectic mixture of different American styles. Some of his paintings are done on a surface made up of pieces of broken crockery, a device which seems to owe a good deal to the work of the Filipino-American artist Alfonso Ossorio (b. 1916), who has married aspects of Abstract Expressionism to things learned from Jean Dubuffet. Schnabel's handling of paint on this difficult support often shows a dexterity worthy of John Singer Sargent, and, when using it, he has increasingly veered towards Sargent in his choice of subject-matter. Many of his recent paintings are the late twentieth-century equivalent of Edwardian society portraits: glamorous images of self-evidently fashionable sitters.

Other paintings by Schnabel are quite different technically. Many are under the spell of Rauschenberg at his most Dadaist. One typical series, produced in 1988, con-

sists of small eighteenth-century engravings collaged onto large canvases, which have been splashed with a few large areas of paint then decorated with the graffito 'La banana é buona'. Schnabel is usually criticized for technical crudity and for trying to be avant-garde at all costs. In fact, his work shows much technical calculation, even where it lacks obvious refinement. It is full of aesthetic ploys which only the initiated will recognize. His deployment of technique is precisely the aspect of his art which does give evidence of considerable cultural sophistication. Unlike European Neo-Expressionism, which often tries to make a political point to a presumably popular audience, Schnabel is content to address the cognoscenti. What he produces is a twisted or altered version of what has gone before which depends heavily on the spectator's knowledge of the original source. It is thus typical of scholarly art throughout the ages – the second phase of Italian Mannerism, for instance.

Very much the same comments can be made about another much-praised artist of Schnabel's generation, David Salle (b. 1952). In a press release put out for an exhibition of Salle's work held at the end of 1982, his paintings were described as being 'redolent of that fridge-raiding, corner-cutting, head-shrinking, violent, messy, clean, sexually obsessed, verbally articulate, quintessentially youthful society' which is still to be found in the United States. Anonymous blurb-writers are not really to be blamed for this kind of rhetoric, and the description does seem apposite in one respect: it paints a clear verbal picture of the kind of thing which many American Pop artists were doing in the 1960s, and suggests Salle's close kinship with them. In his case, the model often seems to be James Rosenquist (b. 1933), whose use of multiple images reappears in Salle's work, often with a graffito-like obbligato or overlay.

Three other American artists have been seen as having affinities with the Neo-Expressionist movement. One is the English-born Malcolm Morley (b. 1931), who is considerably older than either Salle or Schnabel. Morley began as one of the pioneers of Photo-realism, in the 1960s, and in the 1970s gradually developed a much more painterly type of handling. By 1981, when he was selected for *A New Spirit in Painting*, this handling did seem to have some Expressionist characteristics. In fact,

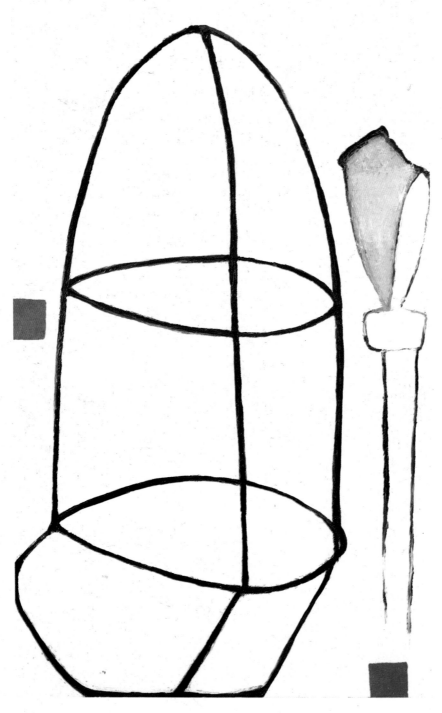

Julian Schnabel. *You Must be Intimate with a Token Few*. Oil on canvas, 243.8 × 152.4 cm (96 × 60 in). Courtesy The Pace Gallery, New York

David Salle. *An Illustrator Was There*. 1981. Acrylic on canvas, 213.2 × 152.5 cm (84 × 60 in). Private Collection

Malcolm Morley. *Farewell to Crete.* **1984. Oil on canvas,
203.2 × 416.6 cm (80 × 164 in). Saatchi Collection, London**

his new work taken as a whole often seems closer to Surrealism than to Expressionism. The pictures are often
conjunctions of incongruous images, rather than logically
and spatially coherent compositions, and many of these
images, in turn, are painted from toys – a procedure
which stresses both the triviality of the enterprise and the
savage sarcasm of the result. Morley seems to be a man
who profoundly distrusts art, who is often seized by
doubts as to whether or not it is a truly serious activity in
the context provided by American society. He is
obviously hostile to the lionization which is now the lot of
the successful artist. And he, like Schnabel, is essentially
a Mannerist; he recycles and comments upon the creative
ideas of earlier generations of modernists.

Susan Rothenberg (b. 1945) has reacted to the strains
imposed on the artist by contemporary society in a somewhat different way. Unlike Morley, her work is not
derived from Pop, with additional borrowings from earlier styles such as Dada, Surrealism, Abstract Expressionism and Neo-Dada. Instead her earlier work was
marked by a retreat into a kind of primitivism which suggests a desire to identify with the very earliest artists –

those who produced the cave paintings of Palaeolithic
times. The horse paintings which established her reputation in the 1970s were at first very close to Palaeolithic
art in style. Since then Rothenberg has gone on to paint
bones, body parts, humanoid figures and, finally, landscapes. In all these enterprises there still seems to be a
search for some primitive essence of experience.

Susan Rothenberg. *Night Ride.* **1987. Oil on canvas,
236.2 × 280 cm (93 × 110¹/₄ in). Courtesy Sperone Westwater
Gallery, New York**

Eric Fischl. *Portrait of a Dog.* 1987. Oil on linen, 285.7 × 433.7 (112¹/₂ × 170³/₄ in). Courtesy Mary Boone Gallery, New York

Eric Fischl. *Help.* 1980. Oil on canvas, 152.4 × 243.8 cm (60 × 96 in). Courtesy Nigel Greenwood Gallery, London

Very different is the work of a major new star of the 1980s, Eric Fischl (b. 1948). Fischl's reputation, unlike that of either Morley or Rothenberg, belongs wholly to the decade. He held his first one-man show in 1980, at the Edward Thorp Gallery in New York. Since that time he has been widely shown in both the United States and in Europe, and his work has aroused a great babel of commentaries. In a sense, this is not surprising, since commentary is exactly what the paintings invite. They are interrupted narratives, or, in the words of Frederic Tuten, who wrote the catalogue preface for Fischl's 1989 exhibition at the Waddington Galleries, London:

Fischl is a painter of fictions incomplete: no openings and closures: all middles… His is the *mise en scène* of psychic turbulence located in what are otherwise considered the centres of the conventional and the normative, the comfortable preserves staked out by the middle class.

Adjectives which have been applied to Fischl by other critics, but without any especially pejorative overtones, are 'sleazy' and 'voyeuristic'.

With Fischl, more than with most artists, one must split the analysis of his work into two aspects – what he shows, and the means he uses to show it. What he shows is, as Tuten suggests, scenes from the life of the prosperous middle class: on the beach, in the street, in the garden, in the living-room, in the bedroom. Many, but not all, of the incidents he depicts are concerned with sexuality, adolescent sexuality in particular. Fischl himself once said that the central theme in his work was:

...the feeling of awkwardness and self-consciousness that one experiences in the face of profound emotional events in one's life. Those experiences, such as death, or loss, or sexuality, cannot be supported by a life style that has sought so arduously to deny their meaningfulness, and a culture whose fabric is so worn out that its public rituals and attendant symbols do not make for adequate clothing... Each new event is a crisis, and each crisis ...fills us with much the same anxiety that we feel when, in a dream, we find ourselves naked in public.

These themes, with their direct references to the condition of contemporary American society, do make Fischl in some ways the equivalent of his German Neo-Expressionist contemporaries. His technique, however, less bold and painterly than theirs, often borders on the fumbling. The notion has been put forward that Fischl's pictures succeed precisely because they teeter on the brink of technical incompetence.

Fischl himself has remarked in an interview: 'I'm still ambivalent towards skill, I'm afraid. I want it and I also want to throw it out.' In various forms, this ambivalence has been typical of much of the American art of the 1980s, and it calls into question claims that American pre-eminence in the visual arts must continue for the foreseeable future. In blunt terms, 'New York style', in its latest manifestations, shows signs of having lost its nerve.

GRAFFITI PAINTING AND RELATED STYLES

The style most closely identified with New York during the first half of the 1980s was Graffiti Painting. It was also one of the shortest-lived art phenomena of the decade. Graffiti artists were, at first glance, related to Pop. Their work could certainly be seen as yet another manifestation of Pop culture. Nevertheless there were important differences between these artists and their predecessors in the 1960s. Almost without exception the leading Pop artists were art-school trained. Their attitude towards mass culture was knowing, distanced and essentially judgemental. The overlay of 'cool', of assumed emotional neutrality towards what was depicted, signalled their separation from their source material.

This separation did not exist in the case of the Graffiti painters. They began their careers as working-class adolescents without formal art training. They were the leaders of a New York teen and pre-teen craze for adding unofficial decorations to public sites and, in particular, to the trains which ran on the city's subway system. What they did sprang directly from the popular urban culture of the city, without reference to modern art or art movements such as Dada. They played a competitive game amongst themselves. Defiance of adult authority was demonstrated by their ability to put their names or pseudonyms on view in as many public places as possible.

These 'tags' or signatures became increasingly bold and decorative, and identifiable styles of lettering developed, often linked to particular boroughs, such as Brooklyn. By the early 1970s ambitious Graffitists were decorating whole subway cars with their designs, and a war of words had broken out between the city authorities and those who defended Graffiti as a new and exciting manifestation of the creative spirit of New York. The first exhibition of Graffiti art – subway decorations transferred to canvas – took place in 1973. By the late 1970s Graffiti Painting had become a staple of the gallery scene which had sprung up on New York's Lower East Side – a symbol of opposition to what was being shown in the established galleries in SoHo and on 57th Street. It proved to be so much talked about and so commercially successful that it soon made the transition to more established venues. The Sidney Janis Gallery, which had been one of the chief promoters of Abstract Expressionism, began to represent a number of young Graffitists.

Graffiti Painting, unlike earlier American avant-garde styles, did not make the breakthrough to international renown. Outside New York it tended to be regarded as an ethnographical curiosity, on a par with Eskimo prints or Zimbabwean stone carvings. Like these 'transitional' art works, it suffered from the disadvantage of being produced by one social group for consumption by another, whose attitudes and values were totally different. As they moved further from their own teen years, and as the graffiti craze itself died away (a decline helped along by vigorous repression on the part of the city transport authority), the work of the Graffiti painters became increasingly tired and repetitive.

The one artist associated with the Graffiti Painting movement who seemed capable of establishing himself internationally was Jean-Michel Basquiat (1960–88). The son of a Haitian father and a Puerto Rican mother, Basquiat had a rebellious early career in the New York public school system and was duly drawn into the graffiti cult, adopting the name 'Samo', which stood for the phrase 'same old shit'. He was different from his fellow-Graffitists in several respects: he came from a background which was at least on the fringes of the middle class; he had considerable intellectual curiosity (one series of his paintings was based on drawings by Leonardo da Vinci); and he also had a notable graphic gift. His abilities won him early recognition, and he progressed through a series of dealers in New York, producing a large quantity of work and generating considerable sums of money for himself and his promoters. It is an indication of Basquiat's facility, and also of the kind of art world he moved in, that some of his exhibitions seem to have been painted to order, just before the opening, in concentrated bursts of work.

Basquiat was almost the only artist connected with Graffiti Painting to make a substantial individual reputation outside the United States, showing in Switzerland, West Germany and Italy; and he was established very early in the secondary market, with paintings selling well at auction only two or three years after they were produced. He attracted the attention of Andy Warhol, who showed his usual keen eye for anything that was at the forefront of fashion and innovation. Warhol and Basquiat eventually produced a series of collaborative works.

Jean-Michel Basquiat. *Untitled*. 1984. Acrylic and mixed media
on canvas, 167.6 × 152.4 cm (66 × 60 in). Private Collection

Kenny Scharf. *Untitled-Elroys*. 1981. Acrylic on plastic, 147.5 × 152.5 cm (58¹/₈ × 60 in). Private Collection

Keith Haring. *Untitled.* **1983. Ink and gouache on paper,
109 × 79 cm (42⁷/₈ × 31¹/₈ in). Private Collection**

Warhol's bland images, with their close kinship to billboard imagery, provided a good starting point for Basquiat's improvisations. The younger artist, however, did not have the equable temperament needed to survive success and, like some of the performers who starred in Warhol's underground movies of the late 1960s, he became drug-dependent and died of an overdose at the age of twenty-eight.

More peripherally connected to Graffiti Painting than Basquiat, but linked to it for a moment, was Keith Haring (b. 1958). Haring played no part in the New York teen-scene which spawned the original graffiti craze, and he did not, in fact, come to live in the city until he was already twenty. He studied at the School for Visual Arts, where one of his teachers was the well-known Conceptual artist Joseph Kosuth. Taking art into the streets was a

Conceptual gesture. In 1980 Haring began to make drawings in the subways, using the empty black panels where advertisements were due to make their appearance. The black background and the material Haring used on it – chalk, the quickest and cheapest means of drawing available – led him to evolve a large, uniform vocabulary of graphic signs quite unlike the playful, wilful style of home-grown New York Graffitists. When Haring began to work in a less ephemeral way, this vocabulary proved adaptable to almost any surface, from the traditional artist's canvas to T-shirts. For a while Haring became one of the symbolic figures in the East Village art scene. Adaptability in one sense meant a certain inflexibility in another. Oil paint or acrylics never seemed to be Haring's essential, primary means of expression. His graphic language was not truly painterly, and this, indeed, was the reason why it could be used successfully on so many different surfaces, employing a wide variety of media. It now seems likely that Haring will be classified not as an important painter who continued to develop once the 1980s were over, but as a striking period piece.

Kenny Scharf (b. 1958) was at one time closely associated with Haring. They shared a loft together; and Scharf, too, was a moving spirit in the galleries of the East Village which had sprung up to challenge those in more established commercial locations. Scharf was never truly a Graffitist, though he likes to add wild decorations to ordinary objects, such as radios, in addition to painting in a more conventional way on canvas. He really represents a baroque variant of the old Pop spirit – a revival of Pop Art concerns within the rather different cultural context of the 1980s. The adjective 'baroque' aptly describes the exuberance of Scharf's imagery, but it is also fair, in a different sense, to describe his work as 'Mannerist' – it represents an intensely self-conscious return to artistic concerns which were once treated more innocently and straightforwardly. One can think of Pop or popular art as having several stages. First, there was a completely unselfconscious mass culture which matured during the

Kenny Scharf. *Decisions*. 1988. Oil on canvas, 68.7 × 53.4 cm (27 × 21 in). Courtesy Tony Shafrazi Gallery

1940s and 1950s. Then in the 1960s the work of the original Pop artists removed the innocence of many mass-cultural manifestations which had up to that point been accepted, without either thought or comment, as a 'given' within the American urban scene. Scharf treats not the original source material, such as advertisements and comic-strips, but the work of the first wave of Pop artists of the sixties as the 'given' element. He recognizes it as an inescapable part of his own intellectual context, and he plays ever wilder variations based on these sources. His work cannot have its full impact unless the audience is aware of to what it alludes.

THREE PHOTOGRAPHERS

One significant comment on the condition of painting and sculpture in New York during the 1980s may be offered by noting the success of photography. As a means of creative expression, this rose to a position of pre-eminence it had never previously enjoyed. Two factors contributed to this success. One was the link between the camera and the Conceptual Art of the late 1960s and 1970s. The other was the increased attention paid to the aesthetics of the medium, and especially the factors which distinguished these from the aesthetic theories prevailing elsewhere. The pioneering study in this field was Susan Sontag's dazzling essay *On Photography*, first published in 1972. Photography's rise in status was also apparent in the booming market in old photographs, once an almost totally neglected area of collecting.

The most prominent of the new generation of American photographers was Robert Mapplethorpe (1946–89), whose prestige was confirmed by a full-scale retrospective held in 1988 at the Whitney Museum of American Art. Mapplethorpe's work, and its critical and public acclaim, represent an extraordinary conjunction of social and cultural influences.

Before he won recognition as a photographer Mapplethorpe had enjoyed minor local celebrity status as the star of a notorious underground movie, *Robert Having his Nipple Pierced*, and also as a maker of collages, often highly erotic in content. Much of his earliest photographic work, done in the mid and late 1970s, is a documentation of sado-masochistic homosexuality. These bizarre and, to many people, shocking and frightening images were presented with great visual formality and also with a kind of mocking insolence which made them seem the essence of New York 'cool'. To everyone who looked at these pictures Mapplethorpe seemed to say: 'Are you going to lose your nerve over this? After all, this is *art* – and in contemporary art, how far is too far?' It is not surprising that these early photographs achieved an immediate, if limited, success. What is perhaps astonishing is the ease with which Mapplethorpe transcended his specialized beginnings, and became a charismatic mainstream figure.

Most of his work falls into a small number of categories. There are role-playing self-portraits (in make-up, for example, or in leather); there are nudes, the majority of which are males, many of them black men; there are portraits which feature either celebrated creative artists or people who belong to a small, consciously fashionable segment of New York society on the fringes of the art world (being photographed by Mapplethorpe became as much of an accolade, in its own way, as being painted by Warhol); finally, there are austerely disciplined studies of flowers. The majority of the images are in black and white.

Robert Mapplethorpe. *Rose with Smoke*. 1985. Platinum print, 58.4 × 49.5 cm (23 × 19¹/₂ in). Copyright © 1985 The Estate of Robert Mapplethorpe

Mapplethorpe's work shows a number of significant influences. It is clear, for instance, that he had a wide-ranging knowledge of the photography of the past. The photographers who made an impact on him cover a wide spectrum, but their work is invariably extremely disciplined, not spontaneous. His influences included the turn-of-the-century pictorialists – Baron de Meyer's flower studies and his pictures of the dancer Vaslav Nijinsky seem to have had a special appeal. One can also see that Mapplethorpe had looked at the work of Man Ray and Frantisek Driskol; at the leading fashion photographers of the 1930s and 1940s; and, perhaps most closely

Robert Mapplethorpe. *Thomas in a Circle*. 1987.
Platinum on linen canvas, 66.1 × 66.1 cm (26 × 26 in).
Copyright © 1987 The Estate of Robert Mapplethorpe

of all, at the male nudes of George Platt Lynes. The result is photographs which are a unique amalgam of the challenging and the wholly accessible.

The deliberate, almost hostile elegance of Mapplethorpe's work makes a striking contrast with most New York painting and sculpture, and it was not until the appearance of the cast stainless-steel sculptures of Jeff Koons that it found a partial equivalent. The core of Mapplethorpe's art is the series of studies of black men. The nudes have a glacial formality; they suggest that the photographer is quite indifferent to the personality of the sitter – often, even in full-length studies, the face is not shown. A number of photographs concentrate on body-parts – a torso, an arm, even a penis. The coldness intensifies the erotic charge.

Mapplethorpe's work succeeds, and retains its avantgarde credentials despite its accessibility, because it touches upon so many difficult issues and subverts so many cherished assumptions. It is in many ways nostalgic, but it shows no sign of nervousness or apology for this. Its racial attitudes are questionable – Mapplethorpe treats his blacks as beautiful animals, not as fellow human beings. The kind of sexuality he celebrates has now acquired an even more dubious overtone than it possessed previously, following the appearance of the Aids epidemic; and Gay Liberation, with whose wilder fringes Mapplethorpe's early work was often identified, is everywhere in retreat. Despite all of these negative factors, Mapplethorpe's work has not only been immensely successful within the New York milieu, to which in any case it owes so much, but it has also been a major cultural export and has appeared in museum shows all over the world. He is now one of the most widely exhibited of contemporary New York artists.

Two other New York-identified photographers of some importance are Bruce Weber (b.1946) and Cindy Sherman (b.1945). Weber, like Mapplethorpe, celebrates the male body. As with Mapplethorpe, there is a strong element of the nostalgic in what he does; he too seems to owe something to George Platt Lynes; and he too is in thrall to the 1930s. His portraits of American athletes, produced in the run-up to the Los Angeles Olympics of 1984, are reminiscent of some of the images in Leni Riefenstahl's famous film of the Berlin Olympics of 1936. Weber is more journalistic than Mapplethorpe – he has done work for Warhol's *Interview* magazine and a good deal of fashion photography. Compared with Mapplethorpe, he usually looks rather timid and sentimental. He is a gifted creator of images, extremely responsive to the cultural climate of his times, rather than someone truly authoritative.

Cindy Sherman's reputation is based on large Cibachrome photographs ($72 \times 47^{1}/_{2}$ inches is a not uncommon size), nearly all of which are self-portraits. The roles she adopts are so various and her use of make-up and disguise so proficient, that it is often difficult to recognize that these are all likenesses of the same individual. In Volume IV of *Art of Our Time* (the catalogue of part of the immense Saatchi Collection), Mark Rosenthal remarks that:

Formally, Sherman's photographs have more to do with the history of painting than that of photography. She often employs mannerist or baroque lighting effects and compositions, and her love of textural play and detail reflects an attention to surface and detail such as might be found in a work by Velázquez or Matisse. Even her concentration on the subject of women is in keeping with the history of painting.

A lot of awkward questions could be asked about this encomium. For example, are Velázquez and Matisse really notable for their love of detail? Has photography in general been indifferent to the subject of women? The really significant thing, however, is the effort to separate

Cindy Sherman. *Untitled*. 1985. Colour photograph, 152.4 × 101.6 cm (60 × 40 in). Courtesy Metro Pictures, New York

Sherman's work from the rest of photography and turn it into something which is quite different in kind. The futility of the effort is demonstrated by something Rosenthal says only a couple of paragraphs later:

... the photographs possess the spirit of the 1940s and 1950s. Yet, although each appears familiar, as if taken directly from a well-known movie, television drama or advertisement, it is a product of Sherman's subtle absorption and adaptation of these sources.

The general drift of this is clear: Sherman's roots are in the photography of the immediate past and in its offshoots in the cinema and in television. The weak spots in her work are not only its rather humourless self-absorption but also its pretentiousness. One suspects that the claim to be different *in kind* from the rest of contemporary photography must emanate finally from the artist herself. Her nervousness about the status of the medium she uses does her no credit.

Sherman's work seems to be the termination of a long process covering three decades. First, the discovery and exploration of mass culture associated with the Pop Art of the 1960s; then the Conceptual formation of major issues (in this case personal identity and feminism) typical of much art in the 1970s; and finally the return to the photographic medium as a thing in itself, and not just as the humble tool which it remained for both Pop and Conceptual artists, who were happy to use the camera but resistant to the idea that it had any special qualities of its own.

POST-GRAFFITI ART IN NEW YORK

It was natural that the New York art scene should make a more serious effort to reassert its international pre-eminence than could be effected through supporting the Graffiti painters. The art which came to prominence during the second half of the 1980s had a more conventional background – the artists were middle-class and from art school. It was also highly conscious of its own heritage – its roots in the immediate past of American art, and in the history of modernism in general. It owed a good deal to Pop, something to Dada and Neo-Dada, and also much to various aspects of the Conceptual Art which had flourished in the late 1960s and the 1970s.

This new art made a number of assumptions which could not have been made with such confidence in any other milieu – for example, that there was already a large and steady audience for all avant-garde manifestations in the arts; and that this audience was thoroughly versed in the history of modernism from the 1940s onwards, and

attuned to the debate about the nature of visual representation begun by Roy Lichtenstein's comic-strip translations of earlier modernist styles such as Cubism, and continued by Photo-Realist imitations of photography. Unlike the European audience, however, this New York equivalent was largely apolitical. The politics it was most passionate about were those of the art world, a cosmos which it thought of as possessing an existence quite independent of and separate from the rest of America.

One result of these preoccupations and assumptions was a return to abstraction. New York art was thus sharply opposed to what was taking place in Europe, or even in most of the rest of the United States. Examples of this new interest in abstraction were the work of Philip Taaffe (b. 1955), Peter Schuyff (b. 1956) and Peter Halley (b. 1953). Taaffe parodied aspects of 1960s Op Art; Schuyff moved to a version of Op from a version of the Biomorphic Surrealism (Arp, Tanguy, etc.) popular in

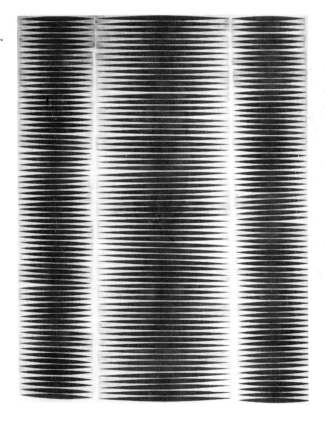

Peter Schuyff. *The Weld*. 1985. Acrylic on linen, 304.8 × 304.8 cm (120 × 120 in). Saatchi Collection, London

Philip Taaffe. *Untitled*. 1984. Linoprint, collage, acrylic on paper, 189 × 150 cm (74³/₄ × 98³/₄ in). Saatchi Collection, London

the 1930s; while Halley, whose work seemed to owe more than a little to that of Josef Albers, took a nostalgic look at the sensibility of the Bauhaus.

Of the three artists just named, it is Halley who currently seems the most interesting. One reason for this is that his work, in addition to having roots in the history of modernism, is equally firmly rooted in the ecology of New York, and in particular owes much to its characteristic architecture – itself the ultimate, corrupted product of the success achieved by leading Bauhaus architects during their years of American exile, from the mid-1930s onwards. Like many of the New York artists of his own generation, Halley is articulate. He says, for example, that he wanted to alter the meanings usually attached to the square, a form which is a basic signifier in certain forms of modern art:

I felt I could use the square as an example of how to take these meanings and change them into other meanings. I wanted to change the square as being abstract and purely unrelated to the world, and posit it as having some kind of physical reality in the world. I wanted to take the idea of rationality as being something positive and re-examine it as either being negative, or at least worth examining as something other than positive. Finally, the square is one of those geometric forms we think of as an ahistorical, a priori mental structure – and I wanted to look at it as an historical structure that has had specific historical uses.

Halley adds to this:

One of the initial motivations in my work is that when I first came to New York, I was so fascinated by facades and decoration. If you went into an office building everything was covered with marble, or wood panelling, or what have you. And I was fascinated by the idea that the conduits, the supportive structure, was always hidden. I thought to some extent this was a

Haim Steinbach. *No Wires, No Power Cord*. 1986. Mixed media construction, 73.7 × 118 × 47cm (29 × 46¹/₂ × 18¹/₂ in). Courtesy Sonnabend Gallery, New York

Philip Taaffe. *Banded Enclosure*. 1988. Mixed media on canvas,
345.4 × 396.2 cm (136 × 156 in). Courtesy Pat Hearn Gallery,
New York

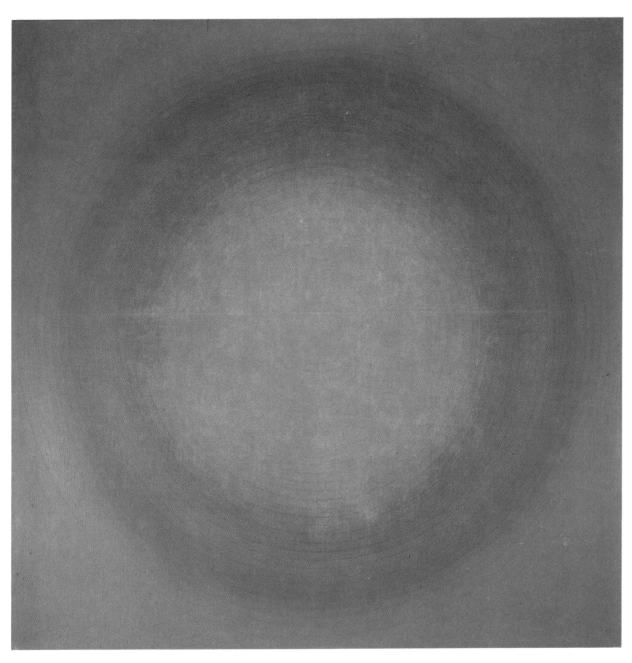

Peter Schuyff. *Untitled*. 1988. Acrylic on linen, 190.5 × 190.5 cm
75 × 75 in). Courtesy Pat Hearn Gallery, New York

Jeff Koons. *Rabbit 1986.* **Cast stainless steel, 104.2 × 48.3 × 30.5 cm (41 × 19 × 12 in). Saatchi Collection, London**

characteristic of contemporary society, and of capitalism in general. I aspired to actually ferret out and bring forward some of those structural conditions that exist behind the facades, if you will.

This is in fact one of the few examples that I know of a directly political comment emanating from an artist of this group. It would be very difficult to deduce any kind of political content from Halley's paintings taken in isolation.

It is clear, however, that this generation of New York artists remains fascinated in a more general sense by the consumer society, whose beneficiaries they are; and that their relationship to it is even more ambiguous than that of the American Pop artists of the 1960s. Most of the Pop artists transformed consumer images when they put them to use. An outstanding example of this process of transformation is the soft sculpture of Claes Oldenburg – giant versions of electric egg-beaters made of vinyl stuffed with kapok, and allowed to hang and loll in shapes which are visceral and phallic rather than hard and mechanical like the original objects.

Andy Warhol was the one leading Pop artist who did not transform consumer objects but took pains to imitate them exactly, in an early series of cartoons for Brillo soap pads. Warhol is the direct ancestor of a whole series of three-dimensional works recently made in New York. Examples are the vacuum cleaners in plexiglass cases 'made' by Jeff Koons (b. 1955), and the baskets, sneakers, footballs and other objects on plinths presented by Haim Steinbach (b. 1944). But these works differ from Warhol's boxes because the main components are not imitations – they are things selected from the surrounding environment in the same way that Marcel Duchamp once chose his now-classic found objects – the *Bottlerack* and the *Fountain* (which was in fact a urinal). All that separates Koons and Steinbach from Duchamp is a nuance. Duchamp's objects were intended as a mockery of the high-art pretensions of his contemporaries – avant-gardists even more than academic artists. In the case of these successors it is not certain that any mockery is intended. If so, the target may well be Duchamp himself, whose most potently rebellious ideas have been so effortlessly absorbed and recycled *ad nauseam* by members of the post-World War II mainstream.

If any one member of the New York avant-garde has succeeded in producing a totem artwork – something which sums up the sensibility of a particular group of artists at a particular moment – this achievement must be attributed to Koons. The work in question is in some ways atypical of his production. *Rabbit 1986* is a sculpture made in cast stainless steel. The 'original' on which this sculpture is based is a novelty balloon, whose soft distended forms have been reproduced exactly in this most recalcitrant of materials. The piece belongs to a whole series of sculptures by Koons which use the same medium. All reproduce pre-existing objects, from a cheap reproduction of an eighteenth-century bust to a novelty decanter for bourbon whisky in the shape of a toy train. All have obvious qualities in common. They are cold and hard; they look consciously chic and expensive despite their flauntingly tacky source material. It is probable that they can all be read as doubly or even triply sarcastic – the victims of this sarcasm being those who consume, i.e. buy, the original objects; those who consume them in the same fashion when they are transformed into high-priced art; and the artist himself, who mocks his own traditional function, which is to re-create reality.

Rabbit 1986 has more impact than the rest of the series both because the shift from one material to another is so extreme and because the simple distended forms of the blown-up balloon suggest a comparison with certain 'classic modern' sculptures – most obviously sculptures in polished metal by Hans Arp, which similarly combine hardness, shininess and apparent squashiness.

By making works of such different kinds within a very short time span, Koons demonstrates an eclecticism which has become an issue in much of the art produced in the 1980s. One of the most dedicated pluralists is another New York artist, Ross Bleckner (b. 1949). Bleckner says:

If I feel honest about making the paintings I make, I also have to allow for certain kinds of mutations within who I think I am. It's how you really speak in a layered way, and how you really are polyvocal. I think that there's a certain kind of confusion or ambivalence in just how and what it is we are emotionally and psychologically, that exists in us all, always, but is never really seen as a possibility, is always seen as a limitation instead. Because I think that, so often, painters see something as having, or refining, a certain set vision. And I don't see myself as having a set vision. I see myself as a human being involved in a kind of productive activity which is almost like the transparent nature of thinking.

Bleckner mimes these 'mutations', as he calls them, in paintings which often seem to shift between genres. Some of his works, like Taaffe's, look like parodies of the Op Art of the 1960s, or of the Post-Painterly Abstraction which flourished at the same epoch. However, a canvas filled with narrow vertical stripes will also sport what looks like a *trompe l'oeil* ribbon rosette, stuck at random on the surface, in complete contradiction to the rest of the design. Other paintings strike a transcendental note, with chalices surrounded by rays or transparent starry globes against a mysterious dark background like a night sky. It is difficult to tell how these apparently solemn images are meant to be taken, when the artist himself

Ross Bleckner. *One Day Fever*. 1986. Oil on linen, 121.9 × 101.6 cm (48 × 40 in). Courtesy Mary Boone Gallery, New York

declares: 'I take all the work that I look at as seriously as I take making my own work, which is only half-seriously. There's a real sincerity and a fake sincerity that have to play off each other simultaneously. I've always said that I'm trying to find the sublime by de-mystifying it.'

Bleckner's work lacks the cold arrogance which emanates from some of what is now being made in New York. But it does suffer from a whimsicality and a trickiness which have also come to seem characteristic of the 'New York style' of the late 1980s. Whether the city can retain the artistic pre-eminence established nearly fifty years ago, on the basis provided by this latest generation of artists, must now be anyone's guess.

Peter Halley. *Red Cell*. 1988–9. Acrylic and roll-a-tex on canvas,
221 × 259.1 cm (87 × 102 in). Courtesy Sonnabend Gallery,
New York

Ross Bleckner. *Examined Life*. 1988. Oil on canvas,
243.8 × 182.9 cm (96 × 72 in). Saatchi Collection, London

AMERICAN ART OUTSIDE NEW YORK

Perhaps the most striking thing about the American art of the 1980s was its increasing tendency towards regionalism. This became ever more manifest despite fierce resistance from critics who continued to base themselves in New York, and the equally New York-based publications they wrote for. The identification of particular art styles with particular areas of America was not in itself new. It first manifested itself in the 1930s, with the movement which was indeed called Regionalism. In the 1960s there was a fresh assertion of regional identity, in the Midwest and in California. In Chicago it coincided with the emergence of various groups of new artists, among them the Hairy Who (1966), the False Image (1968) and the Non-Plussed Scene (1968). Generally these groups have been described as a local variant of New York Pop Art, but the reality was more complex than this.

The new Chicago style had diverse roots. It sprang from European Surrealism. (Surrealist art of the inter-war period is splendidly represented in Chicago's public and private collections.) It sprang from the *art brut* of Jean Dubuffet (shown in Chicago in 1951) and the 'social protest' paintings of Leon Golub. It also sprang from the work of certain local 'outsider' artists, notably the untrained black artist Joseph Yoakum (1886–1976), who spent a good part of his life travelling restlessly as a circus employee or a hobo, and who only began to paint in 1962.

Surrealist and 'outsider' influences are prominent in the work of leading Chicago painters such as Jim Nutt (b. 1938) and Gladys Nilsson (b. 1940), while Ed Paschke (b. 1939) and Roger Brown (b. 1941) show strong traces of influence from the kind of material which also interested New York Pop painters, such as television and comic-strips, but they use these sources in a very different way from Lichtenstein, Rosenquist or Warhol. Chicago art had no ambition to be 'cool'. As Roger Brown says in a statement written for the 'Who Chicago' exhibition which toured British venues in 1980–1:

One of the distinct qualities of the artist in this movement is an intensity, a kind of religious fervor towards their visual concerns as opposed to a merely political fervor which I perceive among artists of different persuasions. Sometimes I think art is really much closer to religion than politics.

Roger Brown. *Chicago Taking a Beating*. 1989. Oil on canvas, 121.9 × 182.9 cm (48 × 72 in). Private Collection

Gladys Nilsson. *Forewarned*. 1986. Watercolour, 152.4 × 102.4 cm (60 × 40¹/₄ in). Courtesy Phyllis Kind Gallery, New York

Sweeden Valley in allegheny mtn Range
near Harrisburg pennsylvania; by Joseph E. Yoakum

Joseph Yoakum. *Sweeden Valley in Allegheny Mountain Range near Harrisburg, Pennsylvania.* **1968. Pastel on paper, 30.5 × 48.3 cm (12 × 19 in). Private Collection**

This 'fervor' may serve to explain why Chicago art already, as early as the late 1960s, paralleled some aspects of the European Neo-Expressionism then struggling to be born.

The artists of Brown's generation enjoyed such an overwhelming success locally that it was perhaps difficult for younger figurative artists working in the same vein to establish themselves in Chicago itself. However, the Hairy Who style was rapidly disseminated to other regions with which the Midwest had historic, economic or cultural connections. It rooted itself in Texas and it travelled down the Mississippi to Louisiana.

In Texas, Peter Saul (b. 1934) shows the same mixture of Pop and Surrealist elements as that which appears in the work of Nutt and Nilsson, while the mixture of comic strip and 'outsider' influences is visible in the painting of David Bates (b. 1952). Saul and Bates, though a generation apart, have one characteristic in common, which perhaps serves to distinguish them from their equivalents in the Midwest. Both are very much narrative artists, and this interest in narrative – in the tall tale well told – can be seen as one of the leading characteristics of Texan art. Landscape painters working in Texas also tend to use stylizations which derive from the art of the Chicago School.

David Bates. *Blue Norther.* **1988. Oil on canvas, 182.9 × 152.4 cm (72 × 60 in). Courtesy Charles Cowles Gallery, New York**

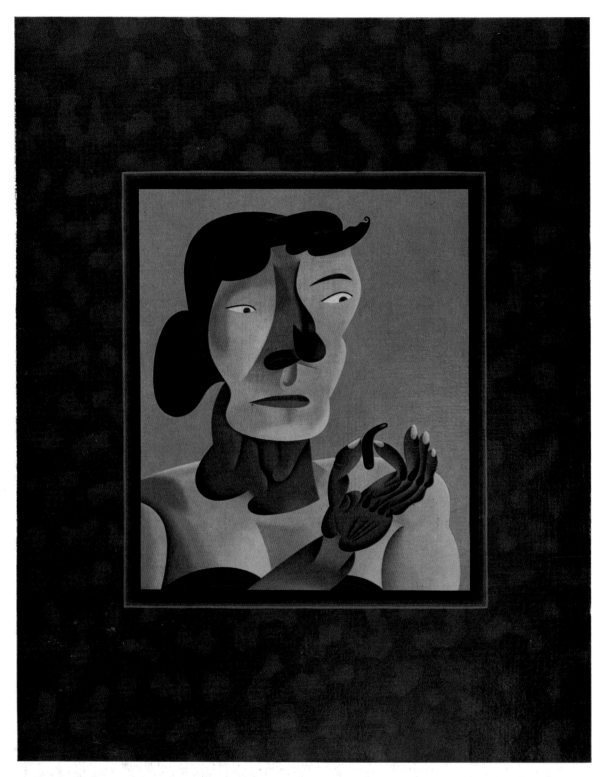

Jim Nutt. *Loop.* **1988. Acrylic on canvas, 65.3 × 60.2 cm (25⁵/₈ × 23⁵/₈ in). Private Collection**

Craig Antrim. *Ravages of Faith.* **1988. Wax, oil, charcoal and acrylic on canvas, 60.9 × 45.7 cm (24 × 18 in). Private Collection**

There is a kinship, for example, between Roger Brown's work and that of Gary Washmon (b. 1955). Washmon was born in Arizona, and received his masters degree in Fine Art from the University of Illinois, but has since spent much of his career teaching at the University of Texas. His work is marginally more naturalistic than that of Brown, showing traces of the original Regionalist heritage from the 1930s.

Louisiana artists often seem to specialize in fantasy. This plays a prominent role in the paintings and painted objects of Robert Warrens (b. 1933), who lives and works in Baton Rouge, and whose work represents the quintessence of this particular aspect of Louisiana art. Folk and narrative elements are especially clearly visible in the objects which he makes as alternatives to conventional canvases.

The most important of the regional American schools, but also the most difficult to define, is that of California. In fact, it consists not of one school or tradition, but several. There is, for example, a clear distinction to be made between the art produced in northern California and that which is made in and around Los Angeles.

One reason for the growing importance of Californian art is the growing wealth of the region, and the establishment during the 1980s of a museum infrastructure which had been lacking up to that point, especially in Los Angeles. Los Angeles now has three major institutional

showcases – the Museum of Contemporary Art designed by Isozaki; the vast Temporary Contemporary (a converted police garage); and the new wing of the Los Angeles County Museum devoted to modern and contemporary art. This by no means exhausts the list of museums in the area – the Newport Harbor Art Museum in Newport Beach, for instance, also runs an innovative programme of contemporary exhibitions. There is a growing number of commercial galleries which specialize in contemporary art in Los Angeles itself and also in Santa Monica, where a stretch of Colorado Avenue is developing into the kind of densely packed gallery area that Los Angeles always lacked previously. In addition, Los Angeles now plays host to a major annual art fair. The fact that the city is in the process of becoming an important international art centre has brought increased respect, as well as many additional opportunities, to local artists.

The distinction between northern and southern Californian art is easier to draw if one looks first at the region in the north, around San Francisco. Perhaps the most striking characteristic of the painting and sculpture of this area is its continuing close alliance to the craft traditions which have always been powerful there. For instance, San Francisco has long been a prominent centre for the production of ceramic sculpture – among the leading practitioners are Robert Arneson and Viola Frey (see pp. 100, 102–3). When it first made its appearance, such sculpture was closely linked to the Funk Art movement which flourished in the Bay area during the 1960s. Funk, from the adjective 'funky' which originally meant simply 'smelly' and which later became a jive or hip-talk term meaning strange or *outré*, meant art which was bizarre and often in deliberate bad taste. Funk had strong stylistic connections with the Hairy Who and other similar Chicago groups, but was more fantastic and contained more autobiographical narrative. Much of the most typical San

Joan Brown. *In the Studio.* **1984. Enamel and acrylic on canvas, 243.8 × 198 cm (96 × 78 in). Courtesy Allan Frumkin Gallery, New York**

reason for this may be the strength and bold experimentalism of local craftspeople working as 'fibre artists'. These have completely broken the boundaries of traditional weaving and papermaking techniques and create some of the subtlest abstract patterning now being produced in the United States. They are only omitted from this book because they themselves so firmly refuse to be labelled as painters, or indeed as any other variety of fine artist.

Roy de Forest. *Big Foot, Dogs and College Grad.* **1985. Polymer on canvas, 226.1 × 241.3 cm (89 × 95 in). Courtesy Allan Frumkin Gallery, New York**

Francisco painting today continues to have autobiographical overtones, often laced with wry humour. This is true, for example, of the work of Joan Brown (b. 1938) – many of her paintings feature self-portraits. The autobiographical strain recurs in the art of Roy de Forest (b. 1930), locally known as the 'dog-painter' because so many of his works portray canines – he also has a penchant for giant rabbits. Roy de Forest is now best known for his later figurative compositions, but in tracing his development it is interesting to see that his early abstract work is very similar in basic style, and certainly in colour and handling, to that which he has done subsequently; the quirky figuration of recent paintings serves as a kind of 'come on', designed to persuade the spectator to take an interest in other qualities, such as the sumptuous colour harmonies.

In general, however, the most characteristic San Francisco painting tends to steer clear of abstraction. One

San Francisco art is often condemned by hostile critics for being (in their view) kitsch. Los Angeles art has attracted blanket condemnation for being superficial. Few accusations could be more unjust. One of the impressive things about southern Californian art today is the solidity of the local tradition and the wide variety of styles practised within this tradition but still bearing some relationship to it.

The oldest generation of Californian artists is represented by Sam Francis (b. 1923). Born in San Mateo, California, Francis is extremely widely travelled, and he has been influenced in particular by a long period of residence in Paris and by his connections with Japan. But he has,

Ed Paschke. *Maitrise.* **1980. Oil on linen, 127 × 198.1 cm
(50 × 78 in). Courtesy Phyllis Kind Gallery, New York and The
Mayor Gallery, London**

Ed Ruscha. *Woman from History.* **1986. Dry pigment and
acrylic, 152.4 × 102.2 cm (60 × 40¹/₄ in). Courtesy
Robert Miller Gallery, New York**

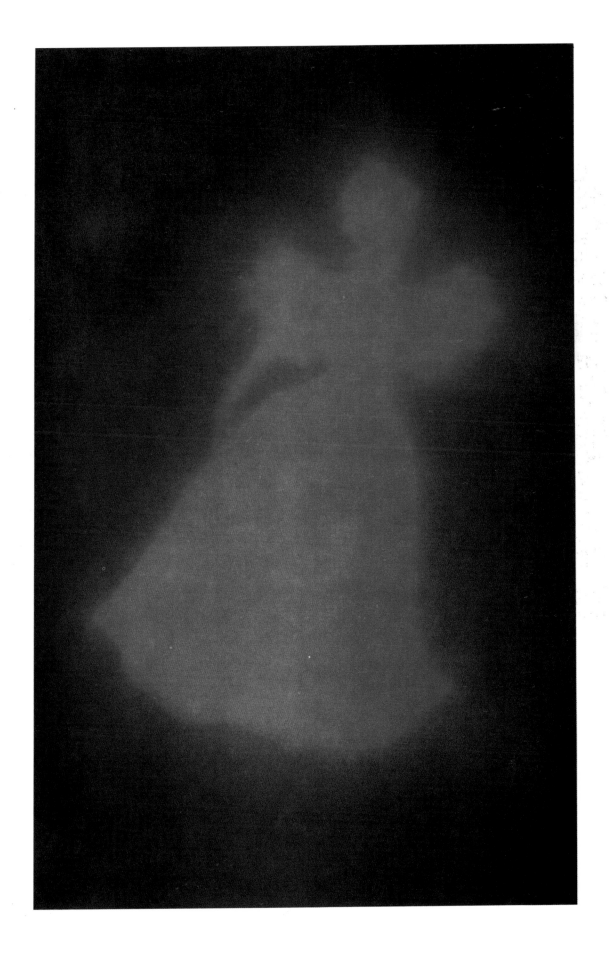

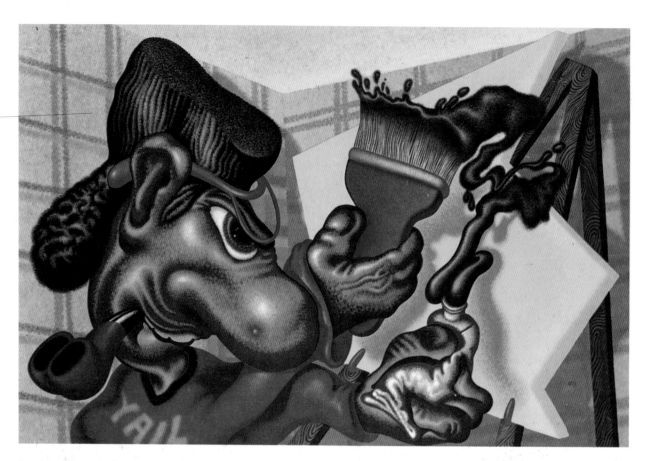

Peter Saul. *New York Painter*. 1987. Oil and acrylic on canvas,
182.9 × 274.3 cm (72 × 108 in). Courtesy Allan Frumkin Gallery,
New York

Roy de Forest. *The Compleat Life*. 1985. Polymer on canvas,
200.7 × 248.9 cm (79 × 98 in). Courtesy Allan Frumkin Gallery,
New York

from the early 1960s onwards, retained close links with California, and the airy elegance – one might almost say the dematerialization – of his style marks his work as being something quite different from the more aggressive Abstract Expressionism of the East Coast.

During the 1960s leading Los Angeles artists maintained a dialogue with what was happening in the East, often interpreting East Coast fashions in distinctly unfamiliar ways. This was true, for instance, of Billy Al Bengston (b.1934) and of Ed Ruscha (b.1937), both of whom owed something to the Pop Art movement without completely committing themselves to it. Bengston, for example, tried to find ways of integrating certain identifying symbols, such as the chevron or 'sergeant stripes', into what was primarily abstract work. He also experimented with materials, using high gloss enamels on dented metal, an allusion to the importance of the automobile in the local environment. While Bengston's work has been criticized for its lack of development in the 1970s and 1980s, Ruscha, originally famous for his sophisticated use of lettering and his high-gloss versions of 'typical' Californian images such as filling-stations, has embarked on a new stylistic phase in the current decade. His most recent all-grey canvases have a subdued romanticism, and seem to look back nostalgically to the days when the most famous Californian cultural product, the movie, made its most significant impact through the use of black-and-white. Even more specifically Californian are recent paintings by Peter Alexander (b.1939). In 1982, Alexander, who had been an abstractionist, embarked on figuration with a series of seascapes featuring sunsets. He thus returned to a theme which had been greatly favoured by Californian artists during the 1930s – so much so that the 'sunset picture' became established as a recognizable local genre. Reviving it, Alexander chose to exaggerate the vulgar aspect of his chosen imagery, sometimes even using glitter paints on velvet. The acknowledged irony is extremely typical of one aspect of southern Californian art.

Billy Al Bengston. *Tangier*. 1985. Acrylic on canvas, 226.1 × 218.4 cm (80 × 86 in). Courtesy James Corcoran Gallery, Los Angeles

In the 1970s, southern Californian art took a new direction, with the rise of the 'Light and Space' movement. Artists associated with this included Robert Irwin (b. 1928), whose softly lighted discs seemed to take art to the very edge of perception, since the artwork consisted not so much of the disc itself but the patterns of light surrounding it on the wall; and James Turrell (b. 1943), who also experimented with light, and in addition made kinaesthetic experiments – for example, one designed to demonstrate the effect that sound has upon taste. At this period (1969), Irwin asserted: 'It is my contention that modern art has been principally involved for twenty years in a disengagement from literate thinking, to place an emphasis on sensual awareness...'

Linked to the concern with light and space as media which could be manipulated in their own right was a more specific concern with the endangered environment. The artists most strongly representative of this were Helen Mayer Harrison (b. 1929) and Newton Harrison (b. 1932). Married in 1953, the Harrisons began collaborative work in 1970, three years after settling in La Jolla, California. In 1972 they started work on what is perhaps their most ambitious creation, *The Lagoon Cycle*, which was exhibited in (provisionally) complete form at Cornell University in 1985. The cycle initially sprang from an interest in a particular species of fast-growing crab, native to Sri Lanka, which the artists thought might be a useful alternative food source. The cycle is divided into seven

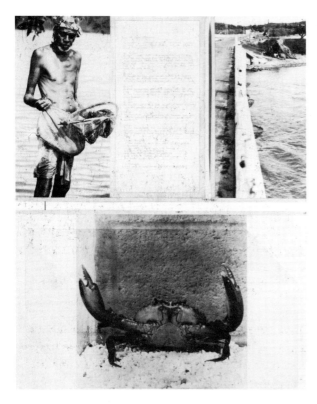

Helen and Newton Harrison. *First Lagoon Panel 7.* **Oil, crayon and photograph on canvas, 190 × 152.4 cm (75 × 60 in). Private Collection**

sections (or Lagoons), and is explained thus: 'The Lagoon Cycle unfolds as a discourse between two characters, the Lagoonmaker and the Witness. The work is named for the estuarial lagoons that are endangered everywhere, the lagoon being a metaphor for life itself.' This work, a mixture of performance, pictorial metaphor, moral indictment and scientific research (the Harrisons were able to induce their crabs to breed under laboratory conditions, which scientists had previously been unable to do), is very typical of the way in which southern Californian art of all kinds rebelled against both conventional formats and traditional approaches in art.

Today, however, this rebellion seems to be on the wane. In this sense, *The Lagoon Cycle* is a culmination, not a new departure. Younger Los Angeles artists are more apt to be content with established categories. What they now have, as a legacy from the 1970s, is a stronger confidence in the validity of their own idiom, combined with a continuing interest in the symbolic. Typical are the paintings featuring crosses and primitive doorway shapes being produced by the painter Craig Antrim (b. 1943). Modest in scale but potent in effect, these seem curiously typical of a culture which notoriously combines a thrusting materialism with a restless search for other-worldly truths.

SCULPTURE

In the 1970s, sculpture, or forms of activity which described themselves as sculpture, was a primary element of avant-garde art. Both American Minimalism and Italian *Arte Povera* were essentially sculptural in their attitudes, and more often than not the artists connected with these movements expressed themselves through work in three dimensions. But during the decade the rise to prominence of new schools of painting offered sculpture a challenge which was reinforced by the shift from public to private patronage. Private collectors found many of the more typical kinds of avant-garde sculpture difficult to house and certainly not very suitable to the domestic environment. Certain sculptors did, however, benefit from the new situation, especially in America.

It is one of the curiosities of the history of modern sculpture in the United States that it lacks continuity – or, rather, that it finds continuity only within a broad stream of development which includes all forms of artistic expression. Thus David Smith, probably the most important American sculptor of the post-1945 period, makes better sense within the context of Abstract Expressionism, a movement primarily concerned with painting, than he does when compared to most of the American sculptors who preceded and followed him. Smith's work provides important indicators for the interpretation of American sculpture in the 1980s, but he is not the direct ancestor of most of the American artists now at work in this field.

An exception must be made in the case of Fletcher Benton (b. 1931) (though Benton's career has been based on San Francisco, whereas Smith is identified with the New York art world). One of the things which Benton has most in common with Smith is the fact that he makes sculpture with a painter's sensibility. At the beginning of his career he was in fact a painter, but in the early 1960s he met a major setback, when an exhibition of paintings featuring motorized elements, and showing images of high-kicking nude female circus performances, was cancelled on grounds of indecency. Benton was profoundly shocked and responded by moving into purely abstract kinetic work. In doing so, he caught the tide of the new Kinetic Art movement, then burgeoning in Europe, and he was hailed as its chief American representative.

Fletcher Benton. *Folded Circle L Ring*. 1988. Steel, 3.2 × 4.3 × 6.5 m (9 × 12 × 18 ft)

For Benton, these first abstract pieces were not really sculpture. What led him to true sculpture was the problem of finding an appropriate housing for the motorized elements of his kinetic works:

The frames started taking over, and becoming more and more dimensional. They gradually became more and more of an object. By 1974 I felt that I had done the same thing with my Kinetic Art that I had done with my painting materials and attitudes: I simply got rid of it… I abandoned Kinetic Art because I felt I had gone as far as I could go with it, and there was no need to take it further.

Buried deep within the new work, however, were ideas and preoccupations he had had when he was still a painter.

Here it is possible to make several direct comparisons with David Smith. Smith regarded much of his early sculptural work as a form of drawing – some early sculptures based on landscape imagery were made directly from drawings which were almost purely calligraphic rather than three-dimensional. Later, when he worked on a much larger scale, it was Smith's practice to assemble the materials he used – metal offcuts and bits of industrial detritus – in various configurations on a flat surface, thus giving a profile view of the piece before welding it together. Though various adjustments were made,

Tony Cragg. *Red Indian.* 1982. Plastic,
320 × 210 cm (126 × 82¹/₂ in). Courtesy Lisson Gallery, London

George Segal. *Helen against Door.* 1988. Plaster, wood and
acrylic paint, 121.9 × 66 × 38 cm (48 × 26 × 15 in). Courtesy
Sidney Janis Gallery, New York

Smith's work is often more two-dimensional than it is three-dimensional, simply as a result of his basic working methods.

Benton has been conscious of this example, as can be seen from an ongoing series which he describes as *Steel Watercolours*, which actually had its beginnings in a series of watercolours made when he was rebuilding his studio and unable to work on a large scale. Other works are made by 'discovering' all the forms to be used within a single flat sheet. Many of these sculptures derive from standard letter forms, a nostalgic look backwards at Benton's early career as a signwriter.

Benton's work differs from Smith's in that he is more prone to invent forms than to find them ready-made in the guise of industrial leftovers. His sculpture is also less romantic, less rhetorical and more playful. What it does have in common with Smith, in addition to its debt to painterly ways of thinking, is its ability to encompass the monumental. Living as he does on the West Coast, Benton has been able to provide himself with the facilities necessary for working on such a scale (now almost an impossibility in New York, simply for economic reasons, as he points out), and he has also found clients with an appetite for large open-air pieces and with the places to site them.

Another sculptor who has benefited from a similar kind of situation, in terms of both working conditions and patronage, is the Texas-born Jesus Bautista Moroles (b.1950), who has a large workshop near Rockport, Texas, and a studio near Santa Fe, New Mexico. Where Benton works in metal, Moroles uses stone – very often the native Texas granite. Moroles's sculptures often allude to landscape imagery, and here, too, there is a real though more distant resemblance to David Smith. In other works, the allusion is to pre-Colombian architecture – something which suggests a link to South American artists such as Torres-García and the contemporary Uruguayan Gonzalo Fonseca. Moroles himself is of Mexican descent.

Moroles, like Benton, often works on a monumental scale. He treats stone in a distinctly industrial way, sawing it into flanges. These deep regular cuts are only possible with the use of machinery. His work successfully straddles two concepts: it speaks of the land itself and of the early civilizations which arose in America; yet it also speaks of the industrial present.

Benton and Moroles, being abstract sculptors whose work is nevertheless filled with hidden allusions to recognizable things and objects, stand between the two camps into which American sculpture seems currently to have divided itself. On the one hand there are the Minimalists, who continue without much variation a style which was already firmly established nearly two decades ago; and on the other hand there is an increasing interest in figuration. One source of the figurative impulse is the continuing tradition of Pop Art, though Pop sculpture has now undergone some drastic transformations. In the case of George Segal (b.1924), it is a transformation of use, rather than a transformation of style. Segal's early work was a form of domestic genre and was unsuitable for outdoor monumental purposes simply because of the materials employed. Since then Segal's concerns have become commemorative and humanistic. Instead of being at emotional arm's length from his subject-matter, he identifies with it, and he has become the sculptural advocate of innumerable good causes such as Gay Liberation. The fragile materials he once used have been

exchanged for more permanent ones, though bronze is often patinated to resemble the plaster he once favoured.

Jim Dine (b. 1935) has dramatically extended his range by moving into sculpture. His early paintings often featured collage elements, and these survive in some of the sculptures. But Dine's sculptures are in general surprisingly traditional – for example, his portrait heads of his wife Nancy, sensitive and Rodinesque despite their gigantic scale. Other works hint at an affinity with traditional Surrealism, among them Dine's paraphrases of the Venus de Milo (shown without her head). In one version, the bronze is patinated in a medley of garish colours; in another, there is a saw which is about to bite into the figure's knee. One recalls that the image of the Venus de Milo also fascinated Magritte.

Robert Graham (b. 1938) has more tenuous links with Pop, though his very earliest works – tiny wax figures in exquisitely detailed environments, often shown under glass domes – certainly had something to do with the Pop ambience. In the early 1970s Graham began making figures in bronze, and this is the direction he has taken ever since. His figures and part-figures – females, more infrequently males, and sometimes horses – are usually

Jim Dine. *Five Heads in London.* **1983. Bronze, central head 287 × 135.9 × 120.7 cm (113 × 53¹/₂ × 47¹/₂ in). Courtesy the Pace Gallery, New York**

Robert Graham. *Spy & Stephanie.* **1981. Bronze, 180.3 × 142.2 × 35.6 cm (71 × 56 × 14 in) & 156.2 × 29.2 × 19.1 (61¹/₂ × 11¹/₂ × 7¹/₂ in). Courtesy Robert Miller Gallery, New York**

Dhruva Mistry. *Maya Madallion: The Dark One – 2.* 1987. Acrylic paint on plaster,
119.5 × 7.5 cm (47 × 3 in). Collection: Tate Gallery, London.
Courtesy Nigel Greenwood Gallery, London

Anish Kapoor. *Mother as a Void*. 1988. Fibreglass and pigment,
205 × 205 × 230 cm (80³/₄ × 80³/₄ × 90¹/₂ in). Collection Musée St.
Pierre, Lyon. Courtesy Lisson Gallery, London

Viola Frey. *Nude Man & Mass Man*. 1980. Ceramic,
172.7 × 233.7 × 165.1 cm (68 × 92 × 65 in). Courtesy Nancy
Hoffman Gallery, New York

Robert Arneson. *Ronny*. 1986. Glazed ceramic, wood, metal and
found objects, 120.7 × 76.2 × 66 cm (47¹/₂ × 30 × 26 in). Courtesy
Frumkin/Adams Gallery, New York

somewhat below life-size and are often presented on tall
bases which form an integral part of the sculpture. The
importance of the base sometimes leads to analogy with
the work of Giacometti, but the comparison which suggests itself even more insistently is one with the bronzes of
Degas. Yet compared with Degas's treatment of the same
subject-matter, Graham's work is conspicuously cold and
often skirts the borders of academic classicism. His immense success with the patrons of the 1980s reflects not
only the positive attraction of his work, but the negative
reactions inspired by other kinds of sculpture.

A number of leading American sculptors, particularly
those from the West Coast, have chosen ceramic as their
preferred medium. Many of them show a wish to demys-
tify the whole process of making art and they are often
interested in the use of colour. Robert Arneson (b. 1930)
was associated with the Funk Art movement. Arneson's
early sculptures were often offbeat self-portraits, and this
tendency continued into the 1980s. *California Artist*,
made in 1982, is an ironic homage to a New York critic
who accused Arneson's work of lacking depth. Dark
glasses reveal a totally empty head; a marijuana plant
grows up the pedestal supporting the half-length figure,
which is shirtless and wearing only a rumpled denim
jacket.

Other sculptures made by Arneson in the 1980s are,
however, deadly serious – they represent the victims of
nuclear war, with the generals and others who are responsible for making war transformed into half-demonic
beings. This is propaganda art of a kind which seems to
look back to Weimar Germany, for instance, to the
photo-collages of John Heartfield.

Viola Frey (b. 1933) makes sculptures in ceramic where
the main influence seems to come from traditional folk
art, rather than from Pop imagery. Her figures are large in
scale, rather primitive in modelling, and radiate a pathos
which makes them memorable. Stephen de Staebler
(b. 1933) creates figurative ceramic sculpture which
is different again. His standing personages are riven,
torn, in some degree fragmentary. They seem wrenched
from some architectural context – relics of a forgotten
civilization. In the 1960s, de Staebler worked with the
leading American ceramicist Peter Voulkos, a great
advocate of total spontaneity in the use of materials, and
de Staebler's work continues to bear the marks of this even
when, as sometimes happens, he prefers to work in
bronze.

One of the most interesting developments in recent
American sculpture is for the artist to use some related
form of activity – something which comes close to art

Siah Armajani. *Element # 18*. 1988. Aluminium, painted steel and pressure-treated wood, 172.7 × 360.7 × 101.6 cm (68 × 142 × 40 in). Courtesy Max Protech Gallery, New York

Alice Aycock ... *Theory of Universal Causality (Time/Creation Machines)*. 1982. Courtesy the artist

Stephen de Staebler. *Archangel*. 1987. Bronze, 302.2 × 67.3 × 87.6 cm (119 × 26¹/₂ × 34¹/₂ in). Courtesy CDS Gallery, New York

without actually being art — as a vehicle for what he or she wishes to say. An example of this is the work of Siah Armajani (b. 1939), which consists of architectural fragments, often in forms and materials which stress that they are not meant for practical use. Another example is Alice Aycock (b. 1946), many of whose sculptures resemble mysterious machines, once again without an obvious practical use. Perhaps the most striking instance of this tendency, however, is Scott Burton (b. 1939). Burton has achieved international celebrity as 'the man who makes chairs'. Every sculpture, whatever its materials, is also a piece of furniture. As Burton himself said to an interviewer: 'In a sense, I'm an impersonator — I'm impersonating a furniture designer. Now I know that will make some people uncomfortable, but I've come to

Scott Burton. *Two Part Chair*. 1986. Granite, 101.6 × 58.4 × 91.4 cm (40 × 23 × 36 in). Courtesy Max Protech Gallery, New York

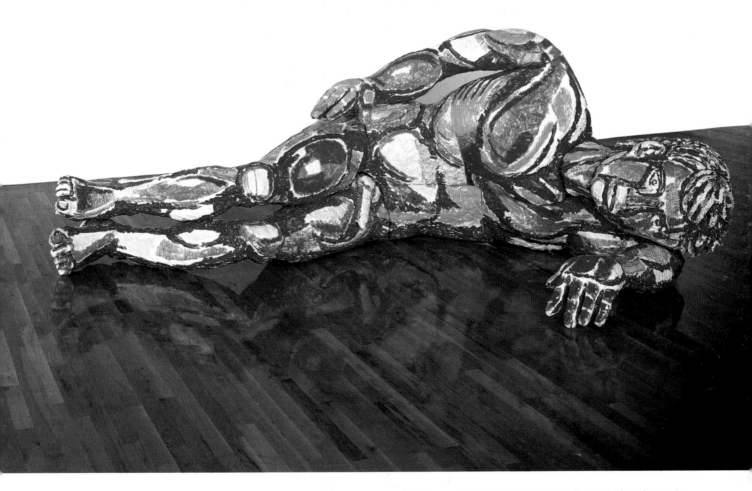

Viola Frey. *Reclining Nude*. 1987. Glazed ceramic,
101.6 × 276.9 × 124.5 cm (40 × 109 × 49 in). Private Collection

Robert Arneson. *California Artist*. 1982. Glazed ceramic,
198.1 × 71.1 × 53.3 cm (78 × 28 × 21 in). Courtesy Allan Frumkin
Gallery, New York

Richard Long. *Somerset Willow Circle.* **1980. 484 sticks, 548.6 cm (216 in) diam. Courtesy Anthony d'Offay Gallery, London**

furniture the way Andy Warhol came to film when he started making movies in the sixties.' The historical contrast is interesting – in the late 1960s American sculpture reduced itself to a minimum, and assumed the unitary forms of Minimal Art. Burton, in the 1980s, goes a little beyond that – he takes sculpture to the point where it more or less disappears. He has even admitted to taking out a patent on one of his chair designs: 'That's a real statement about my intention. The guy told me you can't patent a work of art.'

In Europe, the most active school of sculptors has been the British. This has pursued a different and more coherent course from that of sculpture across the Atlantic. The most significant British sculptor of the 1970s was Richard Long (b. 1946). Long's radical redefinition of the word sculpture, combined with an element of traditional nature-worship, gave his work surprisingly wide appeal.

His most characteristic 'sculptures' consisted of works made on the spot with immediately available materials. Often the only proof of their existence was the photographs Long himself took of them – for example *A Circle in the Andes* (1972), which consisted of a large circle of boulders and small pebbles on a remote South American plateau. These works were evocative in the way that Claude's landscapes or the ink-and-brush paintings of Chinese scholar-virtuosi are evocative. They speak of an infinitely refined sensibility, a nostalgia for remote places and things.

Tony Cragg (b. 1949) uses methods familiar from Long's work – accumulation and assemblage – but his relationship is not with nature, rather it is with industry and the man-made. His sculptures are made not from stones and twigs but from bits of industrial detritus. In one statement he notes:

I am not interested in romanticizing an epoch in the distant past when technology permitted men to make only a few objects, tools etc. But in contrast to today I assume a materialistically simpler situation and a deeper understanding of the making processes, function and even metaphysical qualities of the objects they produced. The social organizations which have proved to be most successful are productive systems. The rate at which objects are produced increases; complementary to production is consumption. We consume, populating our environment with more and more objects, with no chance of understanding the making process because we specialize, specialize in the production, not the consumption.

In a sense, most of Cragg's sculptures seem to be intended as moral emblems of the consequences of production. Some are piles of scrap materials, others are wall-pieces made of plastic fragments (Cragg considers coloured plastic to be particularly important as an emblem of our current material culture). The wall-pieces in plastic are often figurative – one takes the shape of a Union Jack; another that of a Polaris submarine.

Cragg has no recognizable style as such and therefore is not stylistically imitable. But his conception of what sculpture is, or should be, has influenced a number of other British artists. One of the most striking of these is Anish Kapoor (b.1954). Kapoor is of partly Indian, partly European parentage, and his work is related to Hindu culture as well as to that of Europe. Perhaps the best way of describing his work is to say that the sculptures are tantric objects reinvented in the light of European modernism.

One of the striking things about Kapoor's work is its uninhibited use of colour. At first he applied colour using loose powder, but now (for practical reasons) he makes it cling more closely to the sculptures, which often resemble greatly enlarged seeds or fruit. These powdery saturated hues are very much those of Indian folk art.

Kapoor is just one of a group of artists working in England who have been exploring the meaning of the Indian heritage. Some of these are actually Indian by birth – probably the best-known in this category is Dhruva Mistry (b.1957), who comes from Kanjari and whose work is heavily influenced by Indian folk art. Stephen Cox (b.1946), an English artist who has visited India and worked there, is fascinated by the forms of Indian classical sculpture.

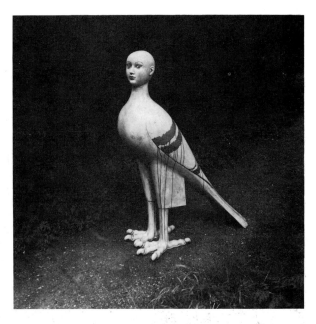

Dhruva Mistry. *Little Bird.* **1985. Plaster, 145 × 112 × 48 cm (368¹/₂ × 248¹/₂ × 122 in). Courtesy Nigel Greenwood, Gallery, London**

Stephen Cox. *Sorgente.* **1987. Peperino, 100 cm (39¹/₂ in) diam., 16 cm (6¹/₄ in) deep. Private Collection. Courtesy the artist**

Other examples of the 'emblematic' way of working –
searching for emotionally associative rather than merely
formal relationships – represented by Cragg and Kapoor
are Richard Deacon (b. 1949) and Anthony Gormley
(b. 1950). Here, too, the work is strongly contrasted in
actual appearance. Deacon describes himself as follows:

I am a fabricator, not a carver or a modeller. In this sense manu-
facturing or building skills are of little interest to me.

Resonance is a central preoccupation. Some issues are relatively simple. I work with materials in the most straightforward
way. I do not make plans. The activity is repetitious. There is no
sense in making things complicated. I begin by shaping stuff,
most recently into circles or cones, and continue by developing
the form. I may have something in mind or I may not. There are
often radical changes. The unexpected happens. I am never sure
whether I finish the thing I am making or whether it finishes
with me.

Despite his emphasis on fabrication, however, Deacon
remains a symbolist in quite a narrow sense of the term.
He has been strongly influenced by the poetry of the great
German Symbolist writer Rainer Maria Rilke, and sees

Richard Deacon. Left to right: *Troubled Water*. **1987.** *Fish Out of
Water*. **1987.** *Feast for the Eye*. **1987. Installation shot, Lisson
Gallery, March–April 1987. Courtesy Lisson Gallery, London**

Anthony Gormley. *Holding On to the Future*. **1987–8. Cast iron
and air, 73.7 × 172.7 × 86.4 cm (29 × 68 × 34 in). Courtesy
Salvatore Ala, New York**

the objects he creates in space as being metaphors for sound, just as Rilke himself evokes space through sound.

Anthony Gormley works in a very different way. The bulk of his sculptural output consists of extremely simplified manikin-like figures, created from moulds of Gormley's own body. The base material used to be plaster, overlaid by sheets of lead carefully soldered together. More recently Gormley has turned to working in iron, but the shapes remain the same. His work might seem to have something in common with that of George Segal, which also depends on making a mould from the human body. But, unlike Segal, Gormley is not interested in anecdotal details – he wants to create a symbolic stereotype. In a number of his more recent works, there is deliberate distortion: the elimination or exaggeration of some part of the body, which makes it plain that the main purpose of the sculptures is symbolic.

Glynn Williams. *Handstand* 1982. Ancaster stone, 45.7 cm (18 in) high. Courtesy Blond Fine Art Ltd, London

Among Gormley's acknowledged sources are William Blake and, perhaps more unexpectedly, Jacob Epstein. His interest in and affinity with Epstein is one signal of a new and interesting development in British sculpture – the return of some of the ideas of early modernism. The standard-bearer of this tendency, and consequently one of the most controversial artists of the 1980s, is Glynn Williams (b. 1939). Williams's development has not been an orthodox one. Even in the earliest period of his career, it was evident that he was a brilliant virtuoso stone-carver. In the 1960s, however, this skill seemed irrelevant, and he was attracted to mixed-media work, to collage, and above all to a kind of radical abstraction based partly on the Brancusi of the *Endless Column* and partly on the reductionist aesthetic which was to inspire Minimalism in America.

By the beginning of the 1980s Williams was ready to return to figurative work. His new sculptures did not renounce modernism. *Two Sisters* (1982) is a homage to Matisse, as well as a tribute to his own daughters. He also looked at the kind of non-European art which had inspired both Epstein and Moore. *Handstand* (1982) has hints of Aztec about it. But his new sculptures were unrepentantly figurative, and the ideas they dealt with were more than purely formal ones.

Williams's change of direction aroused an immense hostility in the British sculptural establishment which is only just beginning to die down. Not the least of his offences was his undoubted virtuosity in handling his material – for his critics, this became almost a proof of vulgarity and insincerity. His example did, however, have a marked effect on younger sculptors, especially those whom he came into contact with through his activity as a teacher, and there is now in Britain a whole school of figurative sculptors waiting to emerge.

It is interesting to compare the development of Williams's work, and the reception accorded to it, with that given to Barry Flanagan (b. 1941). Flanagan first made an impact as a proto-Minimalist in the late 1960s, using materials, such as sacking and rope, which were also associated with the work of the *Arte Povera* group in Italy. By the early 1970s he was already making stone carvings, which featured a rather gnomic figuration. Some were rudimentary forms which hinted at the existence of a figure, others showed a tantalizing resemblance to some natural object, such as a shell. Others were blocks or conical stone shapes engraved with designs. These latter seemed to allude to ancient Celtic art. At the beginning of the 1980s Flanagan turned to making figurative sculpture in bronze.

His figurative work is very different in approach from Glynn Williams's. While Williams's sculptures depend for their effect on his own skills as a carver (though recently he has taken to having some of his maquettes cast in bronze), Flanagan's art is a collaborative effort, as the artist himself was at pains to spell out in the catalogue preface to his first exhibition of sculpture in bronze held at the Waddington Galleries in 1981. This preface read in part:

By the close of the seventies, fashion and aspirations had been continuously qualified by larger external events, and expedients of production put into perspective. The introduction of some concept of trade, drawing on the traditional resources of practice to produce sculpture, became necessary. When out of the garret one no longer works alone, but finds a place in a scheme of things. I am glad to point out that in the production of these pieces in bronze the *work* has been done by others, leaving only the modelling bits to me, as author. Thank you.

Many of Flanagan's early bronzes feature a whimsical image of a hare. Sometimes the hare is combined with another object, such as a helmet or a bell. The modelling is often deliberately rudimentary. The spectator is left in doubt as to how seriously the work to meant to be taken. The material signals serious intentions; the image ironically contradicts them.

Soon after he began working on the series of hares, Flanagan became interested in another theme – that of the horse. He was inspired by the exhibition devoted to the bronze horses of San Marco, Venice, held at the Royal Academy in London in 1979. Flanagan's horses are not new creations – they are replicas, though on a smaller scale, of the antique original. Sometimes the horse is rather crudely married to a monkey, which rides on its back. Here, too, there is a spirit of ironic contradiction.

Barry Flanagan. *Bronze Horse.* **1983. Bronze, 190.5 × 20.7 × 53.3 cm (75 × 79 × 21 in). Courtesy New Art Centre, London**

By replicating an existing and indeed very celebrated sculpture, Flanagan has aligned himself with 'Appropriation' – the label given by American critics to Jeff Koons's replications of pre-existing objects, and also to the presentation of consumer goods as pieces of art, as exemplified by Koons and Haim Steinbach. The ultimate source for this kind of activity is Marcel Duchamp, the inventor of the Ready-made. Glynn Williams's work shows no trace of any affiliation with Duchamp, and though he and Flanagan resemble one another in being sculptors who have at the same moment returned to figuration and the use of apparently traditional techniques (bronze casting and stone carving) there is thus a fundamental difference of aim.

Critics and curators who pride themselves on their support of the avant-garde have found it easier to accept Flanagan's recent work than Glynn Williams's, because the former pays tribute to the Duchampian ethos when returning to the past, while the other refuses to do so. Williams's figurative work has been the target, on occasion, of such extraordinarily virulent critical attacks, that one is forced to conclude that it represents a real threat to the *status quo*.

POST-MODERNISM

Barry Flanagan's replication of one of the horses of San Marco — a classical image — links him to Post-Modernism. This term was not, when it first began to be used, applied to painting and sculpture. It became current in the 1970s as a way of describing a new kind of architecture which was in the process of breaking away from the International Modern style associated with the leading Bauhaus architects and Le Corbusier. Post-Modern architecture had two notable characteristics: it saw the creation of a coherent symbolic language as being an important part of the architect's job; and it very often made a return, if not always in a very orthodox spirit, to the established grammar of classical forms.

The subsequent use of the word Post-Modernism to describe painting and sculpture has been somewhat imprecise. One gets the feeling that the theorists of Post-Modern architecture have been recruiting allies *ad hoc* to serve their own cause. On the other hand, there is no doubt that the 1980s have witnessed a widespread questioning of the attitudes and values of the Modern Movement, and that this questioning has been embodied in works of art which run counter to established modernist expectations.

Post-Modern art can be divided geographically. It takes on a slightly different nuance in each of the three regions where it has flourished most successfully — Italy, the United States and England. Italian artists, for example, have tended to stress the classical element, and it is in Italy that the new tendency first showed itself in aggressive, not to say polemical form, taking the name *Pittura Colta* — Cultivated Painting. This label was invented by the Italian critic Italo Mussa, and was used by him as the title of a book published in 1983. Carlo Maria Mariani was already creating work in neo-classical style in the early 1970s, and Mussa produced a monograph about him in 1980. It is clear from this publication that Mariani's work is rooted in three things — in the later work of Giorgio de Chirico, with special reference to the *Gladiators* and the *Mysterious Baths*; in the Conceptual Art movement, very strong in Italy during the 1970s; and in the neo-classicism of the late eighteenth and early nineteenth century. Mariani seems to have chosen neo-classicism because it was already an art of paraphrase and restatement — it is noticeable that he subtly exaggerates

the characteristics which divide the neo-classical version or copy from the truly classical original.

During the 1970s Mariani was at pains to emphasize the role played by imitation in his work — he made versions of Raphael, Mengs and Guido Reni, and a version of David's *Marat* which included the figure of Charlotte Corday, exiting after her crime. Since that time Mariani's work has become less directly imitative but maintains the mask of neo-classical anachronism. Looking at his paintings, one might well feel, at least for a passing moment, that one was in the presence of a newly discovered canvas by the leading Milanese neo-classicist Andrea Appiani (1754–1817), or a painting by Mariani's declared idol, Angelica Kauffman (1741–1807).

Alberto Abate. *Gorgonica*. 1984. Ink and crayon on paper, 101.6 × 71.1 cm (40 × 28 in). Courtesy Jack Shainman Gallery, New York

Nick Boskovich. *Heart Shattered*. **1986. Oil on paper,**
12.7 × 17.8 cm (5 × 7 in). Private Collection

Stephen McKenna *Two Black Diamonds*. 1986. Oil on canvas,
100 × 150 cm (39.4 × 59 in). Private Collection

Lorenzo Bonechi. *Il Loggiato*. 1984. Oil on canvas, 248.9 × 198.1 cm (98 × 78¹/₂ in). Courtesy Sharpe Gallery, New York

Fassianos. *Ceres*. Oil on canvas, size unknown. Courtesy Zoumboulakis Gallery, Athens

Mussa and other Italian critics friendly to *Pittura Colta* have grouped a number of other artists round Mariani. They include Alberto Abate (b. 1946), Lorenzo Bonechi (b. 1955) and the Frenchman Gerard Garouste. To this list one might also add the name of the Greek artist Fassianos, who also concerns himself with classical themes. None of these artists, however, is quite as convincing in the assumption of a classical mask as Mariani himself.

The mock classicism of Italian *Pittura Colta* returns in different form in the work of the French artists Anne and Patrick Poirier (both b. 1942). The Poiriers make assemblages, environmental pieces and architectural models which evoke the splendour of the antique world. As Anne Poirier puts it:

Our work attempts to reach a certain collective unconscious, or common collective memory. Hence a certain mythology. Like archaeology and architecture, it is an integral part of our mental landscape; it is a veritable storehouse of images. Moreover, like archaeology, mythology is also a metaphor of our mental functions, of the unconscious, and is used by both Freud and Jung.

Anne and Patrick Poirier. *Fragility of Power*. 1988. Polished aluminium, 149.9 × 116.8 × 116.8 cm (59 × 46 × 46 in). Courtesy Sonnabend Gallery, New York

William Wilkins. *Seated Woman*. 1982. Oil on canvas, 230 × 190 cm (90¹/₂ × 74³/₄ in). Courtesy Studio d'arte Cannaviello, Milan

In addition, mythology is an inexhaustible theme of inspiration throughout the history of art. Perpetually reinterpreted, it takes each time a new dimension and can still be used for a long time. But a fable, like history, is only a pretext.

To put it another way, the Poiriers aim to transport the spectator to a dream world analogous to that of de Chirico's *Mysterious Baths*.

It is interesting to compare the attitudes adopted by the Poiriers to those of another French artist – the Hungarian-born Tibor Czernus (b. 1927). Czernus is not 'classical' in the strict sense, but his paintings are, nevertheless, allusions to the past – to art which possesses classic status. His exemplars are Caravaggio and his Neapolitan followers. Czernus denies that his intention is to imitate these artists directly. What he wants to do, he says, is: 'To re-experience the same adventure.' When one considers Czernus's powerful chiaroscuro compositions, the difference which gradually makes itself felt is the lack of specific narrative reference. Most of Caravaggio's mature masterpieces are direct narratives using sacred themes. In Czernus's paintings the narrative is suspended, the dramatic moment left ambiguous and unresolved.

His art is in some ways comparable to that of the Chilean emigré Claudio Bravo (b. 1936). Bravo spent a period in Spain but now lives and works in Morocco. His paintings show the influence of classicism – he is fond of painting interiors with classical statuary – but also that of seventeenth-century Spanish painting, notably Zurbarán. What links him most closely to Czernus is not this, however, but a lack of narrative resolution, and the fragmented sensibility which this suggests.

In Britain, the best-known Post-Modernist painter, often cited as typical of the style, is Stephen McKenna (b. 1939). Like Carlo Maria Mariani, McKenna sometimes paraphrases the art of the past in a way which stresses his distance from it almost as much as his sincere admiration. Unlike the stunningly accomplished Claudio Bravo, he seems to embrace a kind of deliberate clumsiness to emphasize the contrast between his work and that of his classical models. Some recent versions of Pompeian frescos supply a case in point.

William Wilkins (b. 1938) has also attracted the attention of Post-Modernist theoreticians. Charles Jencks, for example, has praised him for the fact that 'Each level of reality is a perfectly plausible world of painting or myth.' Wilkins's art is a fascinating combination of sources and influences. Probably his most important influence is Seurat, and like Seurat he tries to combine the quotidian with a sense of harmonious classical order. A painting like *Picnic*, however, spreads its net much wider than this. Also clearly present are Manet's *Dejeuner sur l'herbe* and

Claudio Bravo. *Man with Turban*. 1988. Pencil on paper, 27.9 × 35.6 cm (11 × 14 in). Courtesy Marlborough Gallery, New York

Carlo Maria Mariani. *April*. 1988. Oil on canvas, 230 × 190 cm
(90¹/₂ × 74³/₄ in). Courtesy Studio d'arte Cannaviello, Milan

Tibor Czernus. *Untitled*. 1987. Oil on canvas, 195 × 130 cm
(76³/₄ × 51¹/₄ in). Courtesy Claude Bernard Gallery, New York

Michael Leonard. *Girl with a Hairbrush*. 1988. Alkyd-oil on masonite, 47.6 × 43.2 cm (18³/₄ × 17 in). Courtesy the artist

Milet Andrejevic. *The Encounter*. 1983. Oil on canvas, 91.4 × 127 cm (36 × 50 in). Courtesy Robert Schoelkopf Gallery, New York

the *Bacchanals* of Bellini and Titian. Painting of this sort presupposes a very sophisticated audience, able to appreciate all the art-historical points being made. Post-Modernism, like Mannerism, is above all else a learned style.

Perhaps the most unaffectedly classical painter in Britain is Michael Leonard (b. 1933). A large part of Leonard's current output consists of solitary nudes, male and female, painted with infinitely refined gradations of tone. The point of each picture lies in the relationship between the figure and the rectangle which contains it. Though the paintings are apparently intensely realistic, they are in fact based on the abstract relationships of solid and void. A similarly classical spirit pervaded an earlier group of paintings which featured scaffolders at work. Here the scaffolding poles were often used to provide the composition with a rigid geometrical framework.

In the United States the Post-Modernist spirit has flourished on both the East and West Coast. There is,

however, a difference in the way that it manifests itself. In the East, it tends to be self-consciously allusive – as it is in the witty paintings of Milet Andrejevic (b. 1925). Andrejevic is perhaps best known for compositions showing groups of contemporary figures in New York's Central Park. The imagery and the way it is used suggests a comparison with what William Wilkins is doing in England – Seurat and Poussin are both present. So too, however, is Balthus, whose early masterpiece *The Street*, exhibited in New York's Museum of Modern Art, has clearly had a crucial impact on Andrejevic and many other American artists.

A classical realist who takes a less ironic approach to his material is Steve Hawley (b. 1950), who lives and works in Connecticut. Hawley is fascinated with technical intricacy, and uses a technique which mingles oil and encaustic. The lustrous surfaces of his paintings are built up using an elaborate method of glazing. Especially impressive are his ambitious still lifes, which generally have an element of *trompe l'oeil* – something which can be traced back to the nineteenth-century American still-life painters William Harnett and John Peto. Like many still-life painters in the past, Hawley is also an allegorist – he is a devout Christian, and the fish that dominates the composition in the example shown here (p. 118) is a piece of traditional Christian symbolism.

David Ligare. *Achilles and the Body of Patroclus (The Spoils of War).* 1984–6. Oil on canvas, 152.4 × 198.1 cm (60 × 78 in).
Courtesy Koplin Gallery, Los Angeles

In California, a revived classicism seems more naturally attuned to the surroundings than it does in New York. The most elaborate and convinced classical compositions produced by a California-based artist are those of David Ligare (b. 1945), who has sometimes been shown in Europe in conjunction with members of the *Pittura Colta* group. Certainly there is a wide range of shared preoccupations, including a desire to find pictorial embodiments for specific aspects of Renaissance and neo-classical art theory. This point is illustrated in *Landscape with a Specific View*. The 'Truth, Utility and Beauty' of the subtitle are the three vital elements which traditional classical taste looked for in art. But Ligare is in thrall to Poussin rather than to Anton Raphael Mengs or to Andrea Appiani, and he is at the same time unmistakably modern. His figures are modern Americans in fancy dress; his Arcadian landscapes have the sharp glitter of Californian light. Once again, it is the sense of anachronism which gives the paintings their piquancy. They acknowledge the cultural fissure which created modernism while rejecting modernism itself.

The mysterious link between California today and the old classical world is further acknowledged in some of the murals painted by Terry Schoonhoven (b. 1945), who in his *Study for an Olympic Mural* tellingly contrasts the skyscrapers of the new Los Angeles (one already falling into ruin) with familiar classical artefacts – the Nike of Samothrace and part of the Colosseum. This link is also mysteriously present in paintings which have nothing overtly classical about them, for example in the exquisite, minute, still-life paintings of Nick Boskovich (b. 1939), who expresses his reaction against American gigantism by producing miniature universes in which everything is in meticulous order. The use of classical systems of proportion is particularly noticeable in some of these – for example in *Heart Shattered* of 1986.

For a use of classical themes and images quite different

Steve Hawley. *Black Glass Still Life with Fish, Pear and Skeleton.*
1986—8. Oil, wax and alkyd, 108.6 × 152.4 cm (43³/₄ × 60 in).
Courtesy Alexander F. Milliken Inc., New York

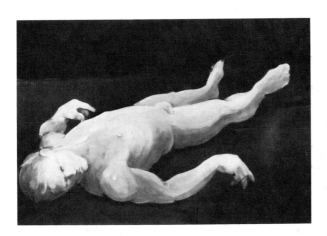

George Dureau. *Fallen Man.* **1989. Oil on canvas, 122 × 177.8 cm (48 × 70 in). Private Collection**

instance, a very strong fascination with the grotesque. The photographs, however, began as documentary studies for his paintings, which convert reality – the reality of people seen in the New Orleans streets – into a dreamlike mythological world, peopled with heroic nudes but also with the hybrids and monsters of Greco-Roman mythology. Appropriately, there is a strong feel of carnival about many of Dureau's recent paintings, and this is combined with a baroque energy which makes some of his canvases the nearest modern equivalent to the frieze of battling gods and giants on the great Altar of Pergamon of the second century BC.

A comparison with the Pergamon Altar seems an appropriate note on which to end, not merely because it fits the work of one artist in particular, but because it was created at a time when art was struggling with problems of pluralism and an almost infinite range of stylistic choice which seem strikingly similar to those difficulties which beset artists today. In the 1980s no one style or way of thinking about art succeeded in dominating the rest, and plurality of styles inevitably led to plurality of judgement – that is, no one set of rules will tell the spectator which artwork is good or important and which is not. More than ever, all artistic judgements became arbitary. The 1980s had nothing even approaching a coherent aesthetic, and all artistic judgements therefore had an *ad hoc* element.

from anything which is happening in Europe, or indeed in New York or in California, one has to turn to the work of the New Orleans artist George Dureau (b. 1930). Dureau has an intense identification with his native city and seldom travels outside it. As a result his reputation has been a thing of slow growth. He first made an impact as a photographer. His photographs combine elements inherited from George Platt Lynes with others which seem to relate to the work of Diane Arbus. Dureau has, for

THE ARTISTS

Note: In spite of all the author's efforts, full information on some artists has proved unobtainable. The numbers at the end of each entry refer to pages. *Illustration references are in italic.*

ABATE, ALBERTO. Italian, b. 1946, Rome, Italy. First solo exhibition in Salerno (1976); has since also exhibited in Rome, Bologna, Milan, Florence, Bari, Alessandria, Trieste, and Taormina. **112;** *109*

ALEXANDER, PETER. American, b. 1939, Los Angeles, USA. Studied at the University of Pennsylvania, the Architectural Association, London, and the University of California, at Berkeley and at Los Angeles (1968). First solo exhibition in New York (1968); has since also exhibited in Dallas, Los Angeles, San Francisco, Corona de Mar, Cal., Akron, Ohio, Munich, Kansas City, San Diego, Irvine, Cal., Santa Ana, Cal., Long Beach, Boulder, Col., La Jolla, Cal., and Chicago. **90;** *91*

ANDREJEVIC, MILET. American, b. 1925, Petrovgrad, Yugoslavia. Studied in Belgrade at the School of Applied Arts and the Academy of Fine Arts (1951). First solo exhibition in Belgrade (1953); has since also exhibited in New York. **117;** *116*

ANTRIM, CRAIG. American, b. 1942. His work has been collected by the Corcoran Gallery of Art, Washington D.C., and institutions in Los Angeles, San Francisco, and Claremont, Cal. **92;** *83*

ARMAJANI, SIAH. American, b. 1939, Tehran, Iran. Has held one-man exhibitions in Philadelphia, Columbus, Ohio, New York, and Kansas City. **101;** *101*

ARNESON, ROBERT. American, b. 1930, Benicia, Cal., USA. Studied at the California College of Arts and Crafts, Oakland, and Mills College, Oakland (1958). First solo exhibition in San Francisco (1967); has since also exhibited in Chicago, Washington D.C., and New York. **100;** *100, 102*

AUERBACH, FRANK. British, b. 1931, Berlin, Germany (acquired British nationality in 1947). Studied in London at the Hampstead Garden Suburb Polytechnic, the Borough Polytechnic (under David Bomberg), St. Martin's School of Art, and the Royal College of Art. First solo exhibition in London (1956). A retrospective of his work was organized by the British Arts Council in 1978. Represented Britain at the 1986 Venice Biennale. **30;** *30, 35*

AYCOCK, ALICE. American, b. 1946, Harrisburg, Penn., USA. First solo exhibition in Halifax, Nova Scotia (1972); has since also exhibited in New York, Cambridge, Mass., and Williamstown, Mass. **101;** *101*

BACON, FRANCIS. British, b. 1909, Dublin, Ireland. Little formal education. Began to paint in 1929, but was not successful until 1945. Represented Britain at the 1954 Venice Biennale. Has exhibited very widely. There have been major retrospectives of his work at the Tate Gallery, London, in 1962 and 1985, at the Solomon R. Guggenheim Museum, New York, in 1963/4, at the Hamburg Kunstverein and the Moderna Museet, Stockholm, in 1965, and at the Grand Palais, Paris, in 1983. **31;** *2*

BASELITZ, GEORG. German, b. (as Georg Kern) 1938, Deutschbaselitz, Germany. Studied at the Hochschule für Bildende und Angewandte Kunste, East Berlin, then at the Hochschule für Bildende Kunste in West Berlin (1964). First solo exhibition in Berlin (1963); has since also exhibited in London, Amsterdam, Braunschweig, Cologne, Eindhoven, Hamburg, Akron, Ohio, Bordeaux, Milan, New York, Basle, Berkeley, Cal., Lyon, Munich, and Vancouver. **15;** *15, 16*

BASQUIAT, JEAN-MICHEL. American, 1960–88, New York, USA. First solo exhibition in New York (1981); has since also taken part in group exhibitions in Lucerne, Kassel, and the Whitney Museum of American Art, New York. **63;** *64*

BATES, DAVID. American, b. 1952, Dallas, USA. Studied at the Southern Methodist University, Dallas (1976). First solo exhibition in Dallas (1976); has since also exhibited in Houston. **81;** *81*

BELLANY, JOHN. British, b. 1942, Port Seton, Scotland. Studied at Edinburgh College of Art and the Royal College of Art, London (1968). First solo exhibition in Holland (1965); has since also exhibited in London, Dublin, Edinburgh, Aberdeen, Glasgow, New York, Melbourne, Perth, Sydney, and Amsterdam. There was a retrospective of his work at the Scottish National Gallery of Modern Art, Edinburgh, and the Serpentine Gallery, London, in 1986. **41;** *41, 42*

BENGSTON, BILLY AL. American, b. 1934, Dodge City, Kans., USA. First solo exhibition in Los Angeles (1958); has since also exhibited in New York, San Francisco, Salt Lake City, Santa Barbara, Hamburg, La Jolla, Cal., Houston, Cologne, Miami, Dallas, Toronto, Washington D.C., Coronado, Cal., Seattle, Chicago, Portland, Missoula, Mont., Thousand Oaks, Cal., Birmingham, Mich., Honolulu, Palo Alto, Cal., Kansas City, and Oakland, Cal. **90;** *90*

BENTON, FLETCHER. American, b. 1931, Jackson, Ohio, USA. Studied at Miami University and Oxford, Ohio (1956). First solo exhibition in New York (1962); has since also exhibited in San Francisco, Brussels, Flint, Mich., Detroit, Portland, Buenos Aires, Caracas, Phoenix, Rio de Janeiro, Milwaukee, Aachen, Offenbach, and Boston. **93;** *93*

BLECKNER, ROSS. American, b. 1949, New York, USA. Studied at New York University and the California Institute of the Arts.

First solo exhibition in New York (1975); has since also exhibited in Chicago, Antwerp, Boston, and Milwaukee. Was included in the 1975 and 1989 Biennials of the Whitney Museum of American Art, New York. **77;** *77, 79*

BONECHI, LORENZO. Italian, b. (as Figline Valdarno) 1955, Florence, Italy. First solo exhibition in Göteborg, Sweden (1984); has since also exhibited in Florence, London, New York, Zurich and Siena. **112;** *112*

BOSKOVICH, NICK. American, b. 1939, San Pedro, Cal., USA. Studied at California State University, Long Beach (1980). First solo exhibition in Muncie, Ind. (1977); has since also exhibited in Los Angeles, Santa Ana, Cal., and Chicago. **117;** *110*

BRAVO, CLAUDIO. Chilean, b. 1936, Valparaiso, Chile. Studied in Santiago with Manuel Venegas Cienfuentes. First solo exhibition in Santiago (1954) and has since also exhibited in New York. Has worked in Spain, the Phillipines, and Morocco. **113;** *113*

BROWN, JOAN. American, b. 1938, San Francisco, USA. Has held one-woman exhibitions in New York, San Francisco, and Chicago. Her work is collected in the Museum of Modern Art, New York, the Albright-Knox Art Gallery, Buffalo, and the County Museum, Los Angeles. **85;** *85*

BROWN, ROGER. American, b. 1941, Hamilton, Ala., USA. Studied at the American Academy of Art, Chicago, and the School of the Art Institute, Chicago (1970). First solo exhibition in Chicago (1971); has since also exhibited in New York. London, Los Angeles, and Atlanta. **80;** *80*

BURTON, SCOTT. American, b. 1939, Greensboro, Ala., USA. Studied with Leon Berkowitz, Washington D.C., and Hans Hoffman, Provincetown, Mass. First solo exhibition in New York (1971); has since also exhibited in Washington D.C., San Francisco, Berkeley, Cincinnati, and Fort Worth. **101;** *101*

CAMPBELL, STEVEN. British, b. 1953, in Glasgow, UK. Studied at Glasgow School of Art (1982). Worked in New York from 1982 to 1986. First solo exhibition in New York (1983); has since also exhibited in Chicago, Munich, London, Edinburgh, Washington D.C., Berlin, Geneva, and San Francisco. **44;** *43, 44*

CHEVALIER, PETER. German, b. 1955, Karlsruhe, West Germany. Studied at the Hochschule für Bildende Kunste, Braunschweig (1980). First solo exhibition in Berlin (1981); has since also exhibited in Düsseldorf, Munich, New York, Freiburg, San Francisco, and Milan. **22;** *22*

CHIA, SANDRO. Italian, b. 1946, Florence, Italy. Studied at the Instituto d'Arte and the Accademia dei Belle Arti, Florence

(1969). First solo exhibition in Rome (1979); has since also exhibited in New York, Amsterdam, Hanover, Berlin, and Paris. His work was featured at the 1988 Venice Biennale. **28;** *23, 25*

CLEMENTE, FRANCESCO. Italian, b. 1952, Naples, Italy. Studied briefly at Rome University. First solo exhibition in Rome (1971); has since also exhibited in Berkeley, Cal., Hanover, Berlin, Sarasato, Fla., Chicago, Madrid, and Basle. Has worked in India and New York. **28;** *24*

COOPER, EILEEN. British, b. 1953, Glossop, Derbs., UK. Studied in London at Goldsmiths' College and the Royal College of Art (1977). First solo exhibition in London (1979); has since also exhibited in Aberdeen, Manchester, and Bath. **54;** *54*

COX, STEPHEN. British, b. 1946, Bristol, UK. First solo exhibition in London (1977); has since also exhibited in Amsterdam, Bari, Florence, and Geneva. **105;** *105*

CRAGG, TONY. British, b. 1949, Liverpool, UK. Studied at Gloucestershire College of Art, Wimbledon School of Art, and the Royal College of Art, London. First solo exhibition in London (1979); has since also taken part in group exhibitions in Metz, Paris, and New York. **104;** *94*

CUCCHI, ENZO. Italian, b. 1949, Moro d'Alba, Italy. Expelled from school aged fifteen, and worked briefly as assistant to a Florentine picture restorer. First solo exhibition in Milan (1979); has since also exhibited in Amsterdam, Madrid, New York, Paris, Bielefeld, and Munich. **28;** *26*

CURRIE, KEN. British, b. 1960, North Shields, Northumb., UK. Studied at Paisley College, and the Glasgow school of Art (1983). First solo exhibition in Glasgow (1983); has since also exhibited in Bristol and London. **45;** *45*

CZERNUS, TIBOR. Hungarian, b. 1927, Kondoros, Hungary (settled in Paris in 1964). Studied at the Budapest Academy of Fine Arts (1952). First solo exhibition in Paris (1964). **113;** *115*

DEACON, RICHARD. British, b. 1949, Wales, UK. Studied in London at St. Martin's School of Art and the Royal College of Art. First solo exhibition in London (1978); has since also exhibited in a number of major international exhibitions. Winner of the Turner Prize in 1987. **106;** *106*

DE FOREST, ROY. American, b. 1930, North Platte, Neb., USA. Studied at the California School of Fine Arts and San Francisco State College (1956). First solo exhibition in San Francisco (1955); has since also exhibited in Yakima, Wash., Los Angeles, New York, Chicago, Paris, Calgary, Fort Worth, Salt Lake City, Boston, Pittsburgh, Philadelphia, Portland, Regina, Saskatchewan, and many Californian galleries. **85;** *85, 89*

DE STAEBLER, STEPHEN. American, b. 1933, St. Louis, USA. Studied at Princeton University and the University of California (1961). Has exhibited widely in the United States, especially in New York and California. **100;** *101*

DINE, JIM. American, b. 1935, Cincinnati, Ohio, USA. Studied at the University of Cincinnati, Boston Museum School, and Ohio University, Athens. First solo exhibition in New York (1959); has since also exhibited in Milan, Cologne, Paris, Turin, London, Amsterdam, Munich, Toronto, Geneva, and Graz. **97;** *97*

DUREAU, GEORGE. American, b. 1930, New Orleans, USA. Studied at Louisiana State University and Tulane University, New Orleans (1955). First solo exhibition in New Orleans (1977); has since also exhibited in London, Laurel, Miss., Atlanta, and Washington D.C. **119;** *119*

FAULKNER, AMANDA. British, b. 1953, Dorset, UK. Studied at Bournemouth College of Art and Design, Ravensbourne College of Art and Design, and Chelsea School of Art, London. First solo exhibition in London (1983), where she has subsequently held two others. **54;** *53*

FETTING, RAINER. German, b. 1949, Wilhelmshaven, West Germany. Studied at the Hochschule für Kunste, Berlin (1978). Co-founded the co-operative Galerie am Moritzplatz in 1977. First solo exhibition in Berlin (1977); has since also exhibited in Berlin, London, New York, Zurich, Amsterdam, Milan, Stockholm, Brussels, Geneva, Munich, Basle, San Francisco, Cannes, Oslo, Vienna, Wilhelmshaven, and Helsinki. **19;** *10, 19, 20*

FISCHL, ERIC. American, b. 1948, New York, USA. Studied at California Institute of Arts, Valencia (1972). First solo exhibition in Halifax, Nova Scotia (1975); has since also exhibited in Montreal, New York, Akron, Ohio, Toronto, and Boulder, Col. **61;** *61*

FLANAGAN, BARRY. British, b. 1941, Prestatyn, Wales, UK. Studied at St. Martin's School of Art, London (1966). First solo exhibition in London (1966); has since also exhibited in Milan, Kassel, New York, Venice, Sydney, Amsterdam, Paris, Cologne, and Chicago. Represented Britain at the 1982 Venice Biennale, **107;** *108*

FRANCIS, SAM. American, b. 1923, San Mateo, Cal., USA. Studied at the University of California, Berkeley, and the Académie Fernand Léger, Paris. First solo exhibition in Paris (1952); has since also exhibited in New York, London, Frankfurt, Tokyo, Berkeley, Los Angeles, and Bern. **85;** *90*

FREUD, LUCIAN. British, b. 1922, Berlin, Germany (acquired British nationality in 1939). Studied in London at the Central School of Art and Goldsmiths' College, and briefly with Cedric Morris and Lett Haines in Suffolk. First solo exhibition in London (1944). There have been retrospectives of his work at the Hayward Gallery, London, in 1974, and a travelling exhibition in 1987/8. **30;** *33*

FREY, VIOLA. American, b. 1933, Lodi, Cal., USA. Studied at Tulane University, New Orleans. First solo exhibition in San Francisco (1974); has since also exhibited in La Jolla, Cal., Kansas City, and Los Angeles. **100;** *100, 103*

GILBERT AND GEORGE. Gilbert, British, b. 1943, Dolomites, Italy. Studied at Wolkenstein and Hallein Schools of Art, and Munich Academy. George, British, b. 1942, Devon, UK. Studied at Dartington Hall College of Art and Oxford College of Art. They both studied at St. Martin's School of Art, London, in 1967, and have since held over 140 two-man and 95 group exhibitions. **37;** *40*

GORMLEY, ANTHONY. British, b. 1950, London, UK. First solo exhibition in London (1981); has since also exhibited in Cardiff, New York, and Munich. **106;** *106*

GRAHAM, ROBERT. American, b. 1938, Mexico City, Mexico. Studied at San José State College, Cal., and the San Francisco Art Institute (1964). First solo exhibition in Hamburg (1970); has since also exhibited in Cologne, Berlin, London, New York, Frankfurt, Dallas, Los Angeles, Houston, Zurich, St. Louis, and Minneapolis. **97;** *97*

HALLEY, PETER. American, b. 1953, New York, USA. Studied at Yale University and the University of New Orleans. First solo exhibition in New Orleans (1978); has since also exhibited in New York, Paris, and Los Angeles. Was included in the 1987 Biennial of the Whitney Museum of American Art, New York. **72;** *78*

HARING, KEITH. American, b. 1958, Kutztown, Penn., USA. Studied at the School of Visual Arts, New York (1979). First solo exhibition in New York (1981); has since also exhibited in Venice, Cal., Rotterdam, Tokyo, Naples, and Hartford, Conn. **66;** *66*

HARRISON, HELEN MAYER, AND NEWTON. American, b. 1929 & 1932, New York City, USA. First joint exhibition in Fullerton, Cal. (1972). Have since also exhibited in Los Angeles, New York, Detroit, Washington D.C., Portland, Williamstown, Mass., Providence, R.I., Chicago, Baltimore, Atlanta, San José, Pasadena, Irvine, Cal., Little Rock, Ark., Ithaca, NY, Palomar, Cal., Toronto, Las Vegas, Wichita, Kans., Boulder, Co., Pomona, Cal., Berlin, and Laguna Beach. **91;** *92*

HAWLEY, STEVE. American, b. 1950, Brooklyn, NY, USA.

Studied Museum of Fine Arts, Boston (1973). He has exhibited in Boston, Mass. (1978) and in New York at Alexander F. Milliken (1981, 1984). **117; 118**

HODGKIN, HOWARD. British, b. 1932, London, UK. Studied at the Camberwell School of Art and the Bath Academy of Art, Corsham (1956). Represented Britain at the 1984 Venice Biennale; the exhibition was later transferred to the Whitechapel Art Gallery, London. Winner of the Turner Prize in 1985. **31; 36, 39**

HOWSON, PETER. British, b. 1958, London, UK. Studied at the Glasgow School of Art (1979), Artist in residence at St. Andrews University (1985). First solo exhibition in London (1982); has since also exhibited in Glasgow and St. Andrews. **45; 44**

IMMENDORF, JORG. German, b. 1945, Bleckede, West Germany. Studied at the Kunstakademie, Düsseldorf (1964), and later with Joseph Beuys. First solo exhibition in Cologne (1978); has since also exhibited in Bern, Eindhoven, Cologne, Düsseldorf, Munich, New York, Paris, London, Milan, Oxford, Zurich, Chicago, and Braunschweig. **15; 17**

IRWIN, ROBERT. American, b. 1928, Long Beach, Cal., USA. Studied in Los Angeles at the Otis Art Institute, the Jepsom Art Institute, and the Chouinard Art Institute. First solo exhibition in Los Angeles (1957); has since also exhibited in Pasadena, Cal., New York, Minneapolis, Paris, Cambridge, Mass., Dayton, Ohio, and Santa Barbara, Cal. **91**

JACKLIN, BILL. British, b. 1943, London, UK. Studied at Walthamstow School of Art and the Royal College of Art, London (1967). Has also worked as a graphic designer. First solo exhibition in London (1970) and has since also exhibited in New York. **36; 32**

JACKOWSKI, ANDRZEJ. British, b. 1947, Penley, Wales, UK. Studied at Camberwell College of Art, Falmouth College of Art, and the Royal College of Art, London (1977). First solo exhibition in Guildford, Surrey (1978); has since also exhibited in London and Liverpool. **48; 49**

KAPOOR, ANISH. British, b. 1954, Bombay, India. First solo exhibition in Paris (1980); has since also exhibited in London, Liverpool, Rotterdam, and Lyons. Chosen to represent Britain at the 1990 Venice Biennale. **105; 99**

KEANE, JOHN. British, b. 1954, Hertfordshire, UK. Studied at Camberwell School of Art 1972–6. Artist in residence at Whitefield School, London, 1987; has held six one-man exhibitions in London since 1980. **49; 49**

KIEFER, ANSELM. Germany, b. 1945, Donaueschingen, West Germany. Studied at Freiburg and Karlsruhe, then under Joseph

Beuys at Düsseldorf from 1970 to 1972. First solo exhibition in Karlsruhe (1969); has since also exhibited in Groningen, Cologne, Essen, London, Freiburg, Milan, New York, Rotterdam, Bordeaux, Düsseldorf, Chicago, and Philadelphia. Represented West Germany at the 1980 Venice Biennale. There was a retrospective of his work, shared by the Art Institute, Chicago, the Philadelphia Museum of Art, and the Museum of Modern Art, New York, in 1987. **15; 18**

KIRBY, JOHN. British, b. 1949, Liverpool, UK. After various types of employment, studied in London at St Martin's School of Art and the Royal College of Art. **54; 54**

KOONS, JEFF. American, b. 1955, York, Penn., USA. Studied at the Maryland Institute College of Art, Baltimore, and the School of the Art Institute, Chicago, First solo exhibition in New York (1980); has since also exhibited in Chicago, and Los Angeles. Was included in the 1989 Biennial of the Whitney Museum of American Art, New York. **76; 76**

KOSSOFF, LEON. British, b. 1926, London, UK. Studied in London at St. Martin's School of Art, the Borough Polytechnic (under David Bomberg), and the Royal College of Art (1956). First solo exhibition in London (1957); has since also exhibited in Oxford, Venice, California, and New York. There was a retrospective of his work at the Whitechapel Art Gallery, London, in 1974. **31; 31, 34**

KOUNELLIS, JANNIS. Greek, b. Greece. First solo exhibition in Rome (1960); has since also exhibited in Milan, Turin, Naples, Paris, West Berlin, New York, Cologne, Athens, Bordeaux, Krefeld, Munich, London, Chicago, Düsseldorf, and Bath. **8**

KRUT, ANSEL. British, b. 1959, Cape Town, South Africa. Studied at the University of Witwatersrand, Johannesburg, and the Royal College of Art, London (1986). First solo exhibition in Johannesburg (1984); has since also exhibited in London and Rome. Winner of the Prix de Rome in 1986–7. **54; 55**

LEONARD, MICHAEL. British, b. 1933, Bangalore, India. Worked from 1957 to 1972 as an illustrator. Held one-man exhibitions in 1977 in New York and London. There was a retrospective of his work at the Gemeente Museum, Arnhem, Netherlands in 1977–8. His work is collected in the Boymans-von Beuningen Museum. **116; 116**

LE BRUN, CHRISTOPHER. British, b. 1951, Portsmouth, Hants., UK. Studied in London at the Slade School of Art and the Chelsea School of Art (1975). First solo exhibition in London (1980); has since also exhibited in Paris, New York, Edinburgh, Basle, Stromness (Orkney), Berlin, and Cologne. **48; 48**

LIGARE, DAVID. American, b. 1945, Oak Park, Ill., USA.

Studied at the Art Center College of Design, Los Angeles. First solo exhibition in New York (1969); has since also exhibited in Monterey, Phoenix, and Los Angeles. **117; 117**

LONG, RICHARD. British, b. 1946, Bristol, UK. Studied at the West of England College of Art and St Martin's School of Art, London (1968). First solo exhibition in Düsseldorf (1968); has also exhibited in New York, Paris, Milan, Amsterdam, London, Antwerp, Edinburgh, Basel, Rome, Tokyo, Bern, Melbourne, Sydney, Hamburg, Zurich, Eindhoven, Athens, Toronto, Bordeaux, Los Angeles, Ottawa, Naples, Dallas, Malmö, Porin, Geneva, Chicago, Grenoble, Aachen, St. Gallen, Chagny, and several British cities. Represented Britain at the 1976 Venice Biennale. **104; 104**

McKEEVER, IAN. British, b. 1946, Withersea, Yorks., UK. Studied at Avery Hill College of Education. First solo exhibition in Cardiff (1973); has since also exhibited in London, Venice, Newcastle, Trieste, Warsaw, Bristol, Glasgow, Liverpool, Oxford, Nuremberg, Düsseldorf, Munich, Southampton, Vienna, Cologne, Stuttgart, Helsinki, Innsbruck, Hamburg, Braunschweig, Preston, Hasselt, and Zurich. **48; 50**

McKENNA, STEPHEN. British, b. 1939, London, UK. Studied at the Slade School of Art, London (1964). First solo exhibition in London; has since also exhibited in Frankfurt, Munich, Brussels, Antwerp, Berlin, Oxford, Düsseldorf, Eindhoven, and Milan. **113; 111**

McLEAN, BRUCE. British, b. 1944, Glasgow, UK. Studied at Glasgow School of Art and at St. Martin's School of Art, London. Formed Nice Style, 'the World's First Pose Band', in 1971. Winner of the John Moores Prize in 1985. **37; 37, 38**

MAPPLETHORPE, ROBERT. American, 1946–89. First solo exhibition in New York (1976); has since also exhibited in Washington D.C., Paris, San Francisco, and Norfolk, Va. His work was included in the 1977 Kassel Documenta. **68; 68, 69**

MARIANI, CARLO MARIA. Italian, b. Rome, Italy. Studied at the Accademia dei Belle Arti, Rome. First solo exhibition in Rome (1973); has since also exhibited in Bologna, Milan, Rome, Cologne, Naples, Turin, Florence, New York, Paris, Munich, Long Beach, and Los Angeles. **109; 114**

MISTRY, DHRUVA. British, b. 1957, Kanjari, India. Studied at the University of Baroda and the Royal College of Art, London (1983). First solo exhibition in New Delhi (1981); has since also exhibited in Bombay, Ahmedabad, and Cambridge. **105; 98, 105**

MORLEY, MALCOLM. American, b. 1931, London, UK (emigrated to USA in 1958). Studied in London at Camberwell School of Arts and Crafts and the Royal College of Art. He held a

one-man exhibition in New York (1968). His work has been collected in the Whitney Museum of American Art, New York. **57; 60**

MOROLES, JESUS BAUTISTA. American, b. 1950, Corpus Christi, Texas, USA. Studied at El Centro College, Dallas, and the North Texas State University, Denton (1978), and as an apprentice to Luis Jimenez. Worked in Carrara, Italy, from 1979 to 1980. First solo exhibition in Santa Fé (1981); has since also exhibited in Dallas, Houston, Victoria, Texas, San Antonio, and Corpus Christi, Texas. **96; 96**

NILSSON, GLADYS. American, b. 1940, Chicago, USA. Studied at the School of the Art Institute, Chicago (1962). First solo exhibition in San Francisco (1969); has since also exhibited in Chico, Cal., Folsom, Cal., New York, Chicago, Madison, Portland, and Winston-Salem, N.C. **80; 80**

NUTT, JIM. American, b. 1938, Pittsfield, Mass., USA. Studied at the School of the Art Institute, Chicago (1965). First solo exhibition in Folsom, Cal. (1971); has since also exhibited in Chicago, New York, Minneapolis, Portland, San Francisco, and Rotterdam. **80; 82**

OULTON, THÉRÈSE. British, b. 1953, Shrewsbury, Shrops., UK. Studied in London at St. Martin's School of Art and the Royal College of Art (1983). First solo exhibition in Oxford (1985); has since also exhibited in Vienna, Munich, Berlin, New York, and London. **48; 51**

PALADINO, MIMMO. Italian, b. 1948, Paduli, Italy. Studied at Benevento School of Art. First solo exhibition in Naples (1977); has since also exhibited in Karlsruhe, Basle, Oslo, Munich, Richmond, Va., and Milan. There was a retrospective of his work at the Lenbachhaus, Munich, In 1985. **29; 6, 27, 28**

PASCHKE, ED. American, b. 1939, Chicago, USA. Studied at the School of the Art Institute, Chicago (1970). First solo exhibition in Edinburgh (1973); has since also exhibited in Cincinnati, Philadelphia, Chicago, Paris, Pittsburgh, and Kalamazoo. **80; 86**

POIRIER, ANNE AND PATRICK. French, b. 1942, Marseilles and Nantes, France. Have worked together since 1970, with joint exhibitions in Paris, Cologne, Berlin, Bonn, Mannheim, New York, and London. **112; 112**

ROTHENBERG, SUSAN. American, b. 1945, Buffalo, N.Y., USA. Has held four solo exhibitions in New York (1975), and contributed to several group exhibitions. Her work has been collected in the Museum of Modern Art, New York, and the Albright-Knox Art Gallery, Buffalo. **60; 60**

RUSCHA, ED. American, b. 1937, Omaha, Neb., USA. Studied at the Chouinard Art Institute, Los Angeles (1960). First solo exhibition in Los Angeles (1963); has since also exhibited in New York, Munich, London, Cologne, Milan, Clinton, N.Y., Houston, Toronto, Grand Forks, N. Dak, and Tempe, Ariz, **90; *87***

SALLE, DAVID. American, b. 1952, Norman, Okl., USA. Studied at the California Institute of Arts, Valencia (1975). First solo exhibition in Los Angeles (1975); has since also exhibited in New York, Groningen, Amsterdam, and Zurich. **57; *59***

SAUL, PETER. American, b. 1934, San Francisco, USA. First solo exhibition in New York (1972); has since also exhibited in Chicago, Los Angeles, Rome, Turin, Cologne, Paris. His work has been collected in the Museum of Modern Art, New York, the Art Institute, Chicago, and the Whitney Museum of American Art, New York. **81; *88***

SCHARF, KENNY. American, b. 1958, Los Angeles, USA. Studied at the School of Visual Arts, New York (1980). First solo exhibition in New York (1979); has since also exhibited in Long Island City, NY. **67; *65, 67***

SCHINDLER, THOMAS. German, b. 1959, Braunschweig, West Germany. Studied at the HBK in Braunschweig (1984). First solo exhibition in Hannover (1981); has since also exhibited in Berlin, New York, San Francisco, Valencia, Paris, Brussels, Milan and London. **22; *22***

SCHNABEL, JULIAN. American, b. 1951, New York, USA. Studied at the University of Houston, and the Whitney Museum of Modern Art (1974). First solo exhibition in Houston (1979); has since also exhibited in New York, San Francisco, Zurich, Chicago, Los Angeles, Amsterdam, and London. **56; *58***

SCHOONHOVEN, TERRY. American, b. 1945, Freeport, Ill., USA. Studied at the University of Wisconsin and the University of California, Los Angeles (1969). First solo exhibition in Newport Beach, Cal., (1975); has since also exhibited in Colorado Springs, Tempe, Ariz., Sacramento, Chico, Cal. Los Angeles, and Sydney. **117; *117***

SCHUYFF, PETER. American, b. 1956, Baarn, Netherlands. First solo exhibition in White Columns, N.Y. (1983); has since also exhibited in New York, Los Angeles, Geneva, Naples, and Cologne. **72; *72, 75***

SEGAL, GEORGE. American, b. 1924, New York, USA. Studied at the Pratt Institute of Design, New York, New York University, and Rutgers University, New Brunswick, N.J. (1963). First solo exhibition in New York (1956); has since also exhibited in Paris, Düsseldorf, Chicago, Zurich, Tokyo, and Jerusalem. **96; *95***

SHERMAN, CINDY. American, b. 1945. Studied at the State University of New York (1975). First solo exhibition in Houston (1980); has since also exhibited in Amsterdam, Missouri, St. Etienne, Tokyo, Amherst, Mass., and Akron, Ohio. **70; *71***

STEINBACH, HAIM. American, b. 1944, Israel. Studied at the Pratt Institute, New York, and Yale University, New Haven, Conn. First solo exhibition in New Haven, Conn. (1973); has since also exhibited in New York, Pittsfield, Washington D.C., and Chicago. **76; *73***

TAAFFE, PHILIP. American, b. 1955, Elizabeth, N.J., USA. Studied at Cooper Union, New York. First solo exhibition in New York (1982); has since also exhibited in Hamburg, and Cologne. Was included in the 1987 Biennial of the Whitney Museum of American Art, New York. **72; *72, 74***

WARRENS, ROBERT. American, b. 1933, Sheboygan, Wisc., USA. Studied at the University of Wisconsin, Milwaukee, and the State University of Iowa, Ames. First solo exhibition in New Orleans (1972); has since also exhibited in Chicago, New York, Washington D.C., and Baton Rouge, La. **84; *84***

WASHMON, GARY. American, b. 1955, Tucson, Ariz., USA. Studied at the University of New Mexico, Albuquerque, and the University of Illinois (1978). First solo exhibition in Georgetown, Texas (1981); has since also exhibited in Lafayette, La., and Austin. **84; *84***

WEBER, BRUCE. American, b. 1946. Studied at the New School, Hun School, Princeton, N.J., and Denison University, Ohio. First solo exhibition in New York (1974); has since also exhibited in Los Angeles, and Chicago. **70; *70***

WILKINS, WILLIAM. British, b. 1938. Studied at Swansea College of Art and the Royal College of Art, London. First solo exhibition in Aberystwyth, Wales (1970); has since also exhibited in Cardiff, London, Warsaw, Swansea, New York, Palm Beach, and San Francisco. **113; *113***

WILLIAMS, GLYNN. British, b. 1939, Shrewsbury, Shrops., UK. Studied at Wolverhampton College of Art (1955). First solo exhibition in London (1967); has since also exhibited in Hull, Sheffield, Leeds, Wakefield, Cardiff, and Bath. **107; *107***

YOAKUM, JOSEPH. American, 1886–1976, Navajo Reservation, Arizona, USA. Ran away from home in 1901 and joined Adams Forpaugh Circus. 1918 served in US Army, France. First exhibited his work in c. 1966. First solo exhibition in Chicago (1967); has since exhibited in Pennsylvania, California, New York and Chicago. Died in Chicago, 1976. **80; *81***

BIBLIOGRAPHY

Art of Our Time: The Saatchi Collection (4 vols). Lund Humphries, London, in association with Rizzoli, New York

Sister Wendy Beckett, *Contemporary Women Artists*. Phaidon, Oxford, 1988

Britannica: Trente Ans de Sculpture. L'Etat des Lieux, Normandy, 1988

Dan Cameron, *New York Art Now: The Saatchi Collection*. Giancarlo Politi Editore n.d., 1988

The Classic Tradition in Recent Painting and Sculpture. Catalogue of an exhibition held at the Aldrich Museum of Contemporary Art, Ridgeford, Conn., 19 May–1 Sept 1985

Tony Godfrey, *The New Image: Painting in the 1980s*. Phaidon, Oxford, 1986

Bruce Guenther, *50 Northwest Artists*. Chronicle Books, San Francisco, 1983

Henry Hopkins, *50 West Coast Artists*. Chronicle Books, San Francisco, 1981

Wolf Jahn, *The Art of Gilbert & George*. Thames & Hudson, London, 1989

Laurel Jones (ed), *50 Texas Artists*. Chronicle Books, San Francisco, 1986

Thomas Krems, Michael Govan, Joseph Thompson (eds), *Refigured Painting: The German Image, 1960–88*. Prestel, in association with the Solomon R. Guggenheim Museum, New York, 1989

Edward Lucie-Smith, *American Art Now*. Phaidon, Oxford, and William Morrow Inc., New York, 1985

Edward Lucie-Smith, Carolyn Cohen, Judith Higgins, *The New British Painting*. Phaidon, Oxford, in association with the Contemporary Arts Center, Cincinnati, 1988

Italo Mussa, *La Pittura Colta*. De Luca Editore, Rome, 1983

A New Spirit in Painting. Catalogue of an exhibition held at the Royal Academy of Arts, London, 15 January–18 March 1981

Mark Rosenthal, *Anselm Kiefer*. The Art Institute of Chicago and Philadephia Museum of Art, 1987 (distributed by Prestel-Verlag)

The Vigorous Imagination: New Scottish Art. Catalogue of an exhibition held at the Scottish National Gallery of Modern Art, Edinburgh, 9 August–25 October 1987

INDEX